HORRIBLE SCIENCE

ANNUAL 2014

THIS BOOK
BELONGS TO:

_____

_____

SCHOLASTIC

DEAR READER...

Welcome to your
HORRIBLE SCIENCE 2014 annual.
It will get under your skin – just like
the revolting parasites wriggling within!
See a heartbeat happen, then pop into
a pongy matter party – and hunt down
the whiffs! Learn a bonkers boiled egg
trick that'll scramble your brainbox.
Discover how horrid humans got to the
top of the evolutionary tree, and make
a manic monster. Oh, and there's
disgusting gore galore, so come and
wallow in the warm red sticky stuff that
pumps round your body … it's really
bloody brilliant.

CONTENTS

GREAT AND GLOOPY GORE

As well as being red and gory, your blood is also very precious. The super soupy red stuff does all sorts of jobs to keep you healthy … so don't let Baron Frankenstein or Count Dracula get anywhere near it!

Some people faint at the sight of it; others, like Count Dracula, can't get enough of it. It's pumped round the body day and night by the heart … but what's it all for?

Blood fact file

NAME OF BODY PART: Blood

WHERE FOUND: Throughout the body in a network of blood vessels. You've got about five litres of the red stuff

USEFUL THINGS IT DOES: Delivers food and oxygen and other useful things your cells need to keep going

GRISLY DETAILS: You can lose one third of your blood without threat to life. But if you lose half – it's FATAL!

AMAZING FEATURES: Blood is so full of things, it's amazing they all fit in. Read on and find out more...

Really red?

Did you know that most of your blood is actually yellow? Spin a test tube of blood round and round very fast and the blood cells sink to the bottom, with a clear yellow fluid, called plasma, on top. Plasma is 90 per cent water, so scientists have worked out how to dry it into a powder – and turn it back into a liquid!

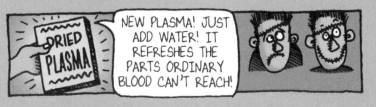

DRIED PLASMA

NEW PLASMA! JUST ADD WATER! IT REFRESHES THE PARTS ORDINARY BLOOD CAN'T REACH!

Super soup

Blood is like a sort of super soup squirting through your body. It's full of sugars and other molecules from your food, which is why mosquitoes – and vampires! – find it so tasty.

AND IT ISN'T TOMATO SOUP!

Rammed red stuff

Blood is THREE TIMES thicker than water. It's swarming with cells! Here's what you get in one teeny little millimetre-sized drop:

• 7,000 white blood cells,
• 300,000 platelets – the little bits of bone marrow cell that help your blood to clot,
• 5,000,000 (5 million) red blood cells.

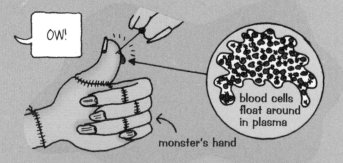

OW!

blood cells float around in plasma

monster's hand

But that's nothing. In all, your body contains:
• 35,000,000,000 (35 billion) white cells,
• 500,000,000,000 (500 billion) platelets
• 25,000,000,000,000 (25 trillion) red cells!

Cells with skills

Your blood supply is like a running track or a road system, teeming with blood cells that are racing around doing many different jobs.

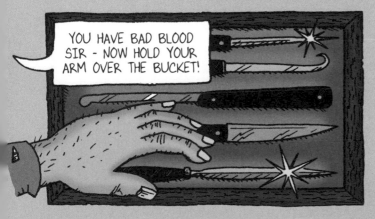

It all starts in the bone marrow, the factory that makes your blood cells. Once they're up and running, your red blood cells pick up oxygen from the lungs and carry it through all the blood vessels around your body. When they run out of oxygen, they get replaced by new cells. The white blood cells are tough protectors of the whole system – they fight off infections and bacteria which attack other cells. Platelets mend the 'roads' – they help heal cuts and bruises by knitting blood together in scabs.

COUNT DRACULA GAVE ME THIS. HE'S A NICE CHAP, BUT HE CAN BE A PAIN IN THE NECK!

Blood-thirsty bleeders

When people are very ill or lose a lot of blood, new blood can be put into them – a blood 'transfusion'. The blood is kept in 'blood banks'. Sounds yucky? Things were a lot more gruesome 200 years ago. Even if you only had a cough, your local friendly doctor might try to open your veins to remove 'bad blood'! The doctors had a selection of vicious looking knives especially designed for this grisly job.

YOU HAVE BAD BLOOD SIR – NOW HOLD YOUR ARM OVER THE BUCKET!

'Bad blood' was a daft and dangerous idea, but things could get worse. Disgustingly worse. But what could possibly be worse…?

How about something green and slimy, with three stabbing teeth … that sucks your blood! LEECHES! Surgeons used leeches on children because they thought it was kinder than cutting the kids with knives. Mmm, thanks a bunch!

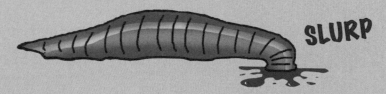

SLURP

The lively liver

Your liver certainly has to be lively – scientists know of 500 jobs it tackles and there may be more that haven't been discovered. It's busy, but let's take a quick look! Your brownish-reddish liver is a close friend of your blood, and works with it in all sorts of ways:

• Controlling the amount of sugar in the blood. This is done with the aid of a substance called insulin which is produced by another organ called the pancreas. Too little insulin causes a disease called diabetes. People with diabetes have to be very careful with their sugar levels and meal times.

• Sorting and storing spare fat and carbohydrates

• Making Vitamin A

• Getting rid of old red blood cells

• Producing digestive juices

• Sorting and getting rid of unused food energy

• Keeping you warm – doing so many things helps to produce heat!

Your liver weighs in at 1.5kg. That's slightly heavier than your brain – and it's pretty much as busy! So look after it, keep it away from Baron Frankenstein, and don't forget, you can't liver without it! (Groan!)

IT'S MY JOB TO DE-LIVER!

LIVER 'N' LET DIE!

Right! Let's visit that racetrack…

RACING ROAD

Your blood runs around your body in a mad marathon race on a long network of highways. Along the way there are many obstacles and accidents, but your blood just keeps going…

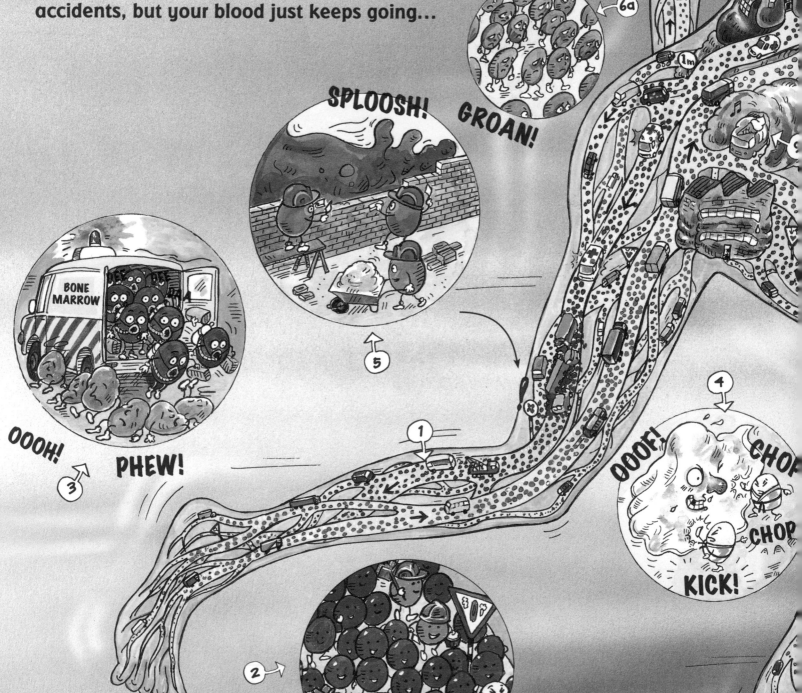

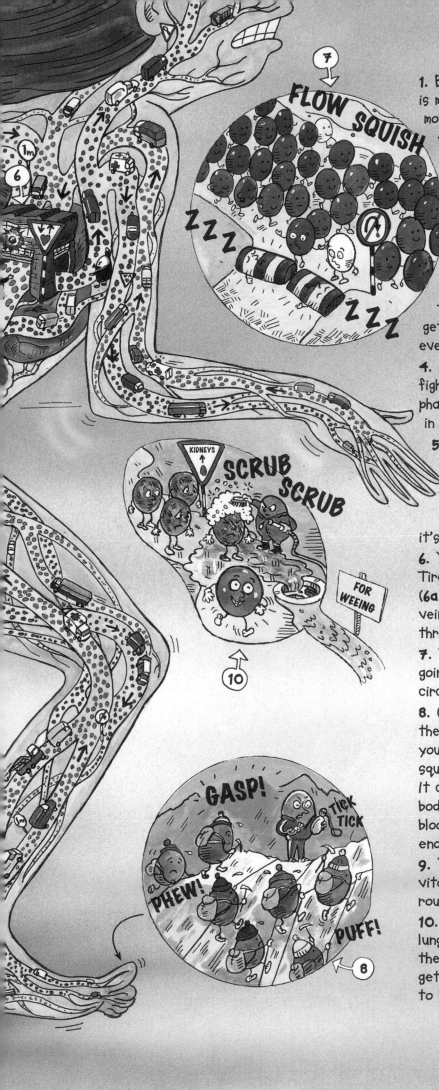

1. Blood is made up of cells and plasma – which is mainly water along with 10 per cent healthy molecules and minerals.

2. Those blood cells are all super busy with their different jobs – and like traffic on a busy road, they have they own 'lanes'. The red cells travel down the middle of blood vessels, and the white ones usually go along the edges. There's no time to stop!

3. Red blood cells carry oxygen from the lungs around the body. The cells are all made in the bone marrow at a massive rate of two to three million every second. Why don't things get overcrowded? Because three million die every second too!

4. If you've got a cold, white blood cells can help fight infections. These include tough types called phagocytes (fag-o-sites) that kill unwanted bacteria in the blood.

5. When you cut or bruise yourself, platelets help clot your blood to stop you from bleeding too much. By releasing chemicals they help blood form a sticky plug which hardens to a scab, acting as a shield over the skin until it's healed. Don't pick at it!

6. Your heart pumps blood around a one-way system. Tired red blood cells feeling blue and out of oxygen (6a) return to the heart along floppy vena cava veins, and are replaced by healthy ones (6b) leaving through big arteries.

7. Valves on veins and in the heart stop the blood going the wrong way. No U-turns are allowed in the circulation road!

8. Capillaries are tiny blood vessels that reach into the smallest, furthest bits of your body, such as your toes. Red blood cells are just tiny enough to squeeze through them, like intrepid adventurers. It can take just a minute for a cell to do a full body circuit, but there's around 100,000 km of blood vessels in your body altogether – that's enough to wrap around the world 2.5 times!

9. Your blood also picks up sugars, nutrients and vitamins from the stomach and intestines to deliver round the body so you don't get too tired.

10. Waste carbon dioxide is taken back to the lungs to be breathed out. Anything else goes to the kidneys where the blood is washed. The waste gets turned into pee, and sent to the bladder to be weed away. Wee!

HARD-WORKING HEART

You just can't help but ♥ your heart. You can't beat it – it's the squidgy, squirty organ that keeps you alive. So don't have a heavy heart – get your finger on the pulse and get ready to know your heart … by heart!

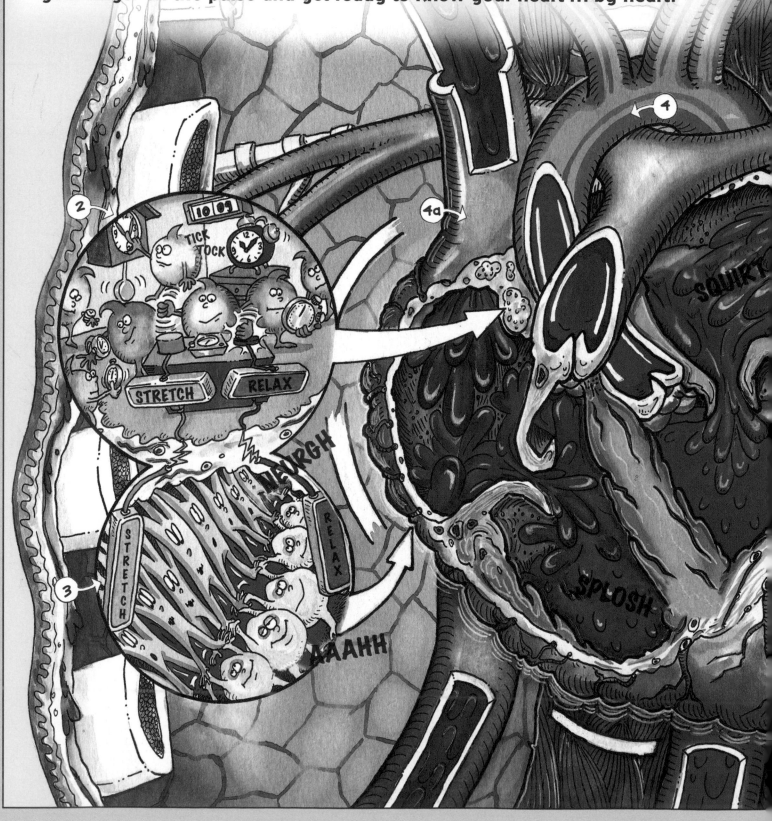

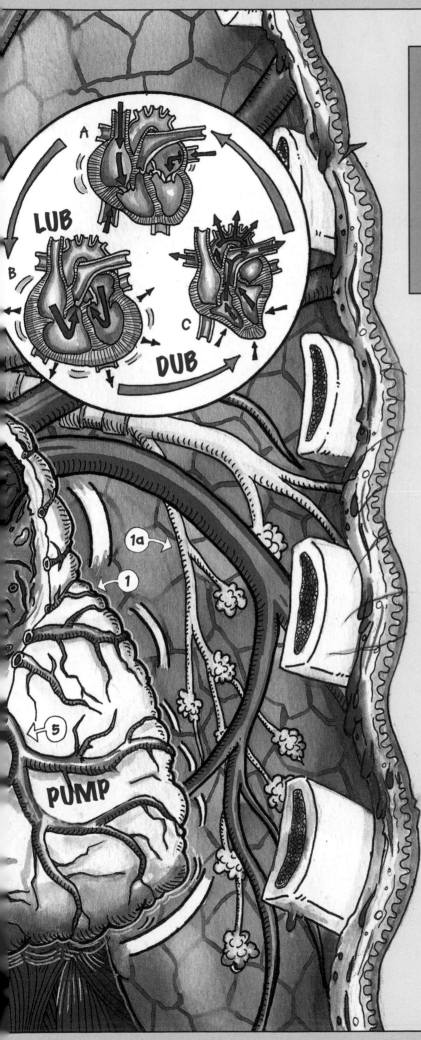

A. Blood flows first into the upper chambers of the heart, known as 'atria' (ay-tree-a).

B. Then the heart pumps it into the larger chambers known as 'ventricles' (ven-tree-cals). As the valves close they make the first part of your heartbeat sound. The noise is known internationally as 'lub'.

C. One last big squeeze from the heart sends the blood shooting out into your body. The right side of the heart pumps deoxygenated blood (blood low in oxygen) to the lungs for an oxygen top-up. The left side sends oxygenated blood to your organs and muscles. The sound of this muscly thump is known as 'dub'.

1. Your heart is a big lump of meaty muscle in the middle of your chest. It's protected by your sternum (chest bone), but your heart sticks out on the left-hand side, which makes it feel as if it's on the left. It is the beating centre of your body. About as big as your clenched fist, it has four chambers inside it and works like a double pump. One side pumps blood to the lungs (1a) to pick up oxygen, and the other side pumps the oxygenated blood to the rest of your body.

2. A small knob of 'pacemaker' cells in the right atrium make sure that all the muscles in your heart (called 'cardiac muscles') flex together.

3. Cardiac muscles are different to the rest of your muscles. They can work continuously without ever getting tired. This makes hearts horribly hard-working. They never stop pumping as long as you live and never take a rest! Over an average lifetime, a heart might beat three billion times. That sure takes some beating!

4. Healthy hearts generate so much pressure that if you cut an artery (the tubes carrying blood away from the heart) the blood squirts many metres. To take this pressure, arteries need to have thick walls. By the time blood gets back to the heart it has lost most of its pressure, so veins (4a) have valves to stop it from sloshing about.

5. The heart needs its own blood supply to feed the cardiac muscles. If this supply becomes blocked by fatty deposits in the arteries, your heart muscles can't get enough oxygen and this can lead to a heart attack.

HOW TO TAKE YOUR POWERFUL PULSE

Your heart powerfully pumps gallons of blood around your body every day, sometimes speeding up, sometimes slowing down. Find your personal pulse rate, when it changes – and compare it with friends.

- your index and middle finger
- a watch/clock with second hand
- pencil and paper
- a friend to lend a hand (optional)

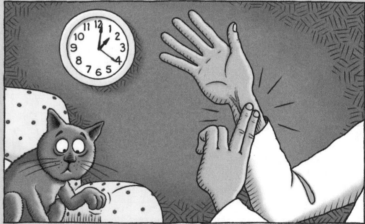

1 Take your pulse. The easiest way is to place your index and middle finger firmly (but not too hard!) on the outside of your wrist. Move it around until you feel a gentle throbbing on an artery. This is called your radial pulse.

SCRATCH

THROB THROB THROB

2 If you prefer, your could feel your carotid pulse, where the artery on your neck carries blood to your head. Gently press on the side of your windpipe, at the front of your neck. You should feel a gentle throb, but again be careful not to press too hard!

MOGGO

3 Now you are ready to measure your normal pulse. Look at your watch or clock. Start counting the number of throbs that happen in 30 seconds. Unless you're very excited, there should be slightly more than one every second.

4 Take the number and multiply it by two. The result is your pulse rate per minute! It should be about 70-85 beats-per-minute. Write it down to keep a record.

5 Now it's time to see what happens to your pulse under different conditions. Try running up and down the stairs a few times, or racing around the garden until you're out of breath. Don't fall over or crash into things!

WHEEZE!

PUFF!

YAWN!

BRRRIIING!

6 Now check your pulse in the same way. Because you've been running, your blood flows faster to your lungs and body, so your heart beats faster. It's probably more than 100 beats-per-minute now!

7 Later try measuring your pulse when you've just woken up in the morning. It might be a bit slower than normal, as you're all floppy and relaxed.

8 Your body temperature can also change your pulse rate. Try taking it when you're in a warm bath, or if you're feeling cold. See the difference!

9 Try taking your pulse in all sorts of situations, such as when you've just had a big meal and your stomach needs more blood to digest food. Try it with friends as well, to see how their pulses compare to yours.

BLOODY DISGUSTING

Still lusting for bloody facts – are you bloodthirsty for more?
Few liquids are as amazing AND gross as blood.
Read on, if your heart's still in it...

Royal Blood

Haemophilia (hee-mo-fil-ia) is when blood doesn't clot properly. Can you imagine what might happen if you didn't get a scab when you cut yourself? There would be nothing to stop you bleeding and bleeding and bleeding and blee... OK, you get the picture. So people who suffer from haemophilia are at serious risk of bleeding to death.

Girls – you can relax, as it is mainly men who get this disease. Mind you, women can pass it on to their children, as Queen Victoria did. She gave it to three of her children. How kind!

The most famous person to have had the disease was Alexis, the son of Tsar Nicholas II (Tsar is Russian for emperor). It wasn't just Alexis who came to a bloody end, but his whole family. In 1917, they were murdered by the Bolsheviks (a group who didn't believe the royal family should be in charge of the country).

Haemophilia is sometimes called the 'Royal Disease'. But it's not really that snobbish – it can affect all types of people. Luckily, it can be treated nowadays with stuff called clotting factors. Phew!

OOPS, MY BLOOD'S 'RUSSIAN' OUT!

GRIME PAYS

In 2000, Italian body experts claimed that dirt is good for smaller bodies. According to them, getting to grips with germs by making mud-pies, being slobbered by the dog, kissing the cat and licking fluffy lollies off the floor, trains white blood cells to remember germs so the body can fight off disease in the future. Experts are still arguing about this although it's a good excuse for getting dirty!

Saw Point

A Canadian lumberjack was chopping down a tree when his chainsaw slipped. He cut his WHOLE BODY IN HALF – except for nerves in his spine that take messages from his brain to his body. A helicopter rushed him to hospital and surgeons were able to sew up his broken, beastly and very bloody body bits. He made it home in one piece.

TIMB-URRRRGH!

SNAPPY AND HAPPY

Which animal has the best blood? The answer might be crocodiles. They have an antibiotic (type of medicine) in their blood, called crocodillin, which means they hardly ever get ill. Great news for crocs, but also for us too! Scientists are finding out about using crocodillin in medicines to help kill nasty germs.

MAKE IT SNAPPY!

What a Clot of Blood!

The largest ever blood donation in one day took place in India on December 7, 2003. A record 15,432 people turned up, willing to give up some of their red stuff. Altogether they gave about 67 bathtubs of it in 12 hours! Fangs off, Dracula!

BATHTIME!

Have a heart!

Your heart keeps you alive by pumping blood around your body, right? So, what happens if your heart doesn't work properly? You get a replacement! Can you imagine having someone else's heart beating inside you? This is exactly what happens with a heart transplant.

Replacing a heart is no simple task. For a start you need a healthy heart that is no longer needed by its owner (in other words, its owner must have recently died). Then you have just four hours to get the heart from the old owner to the new owner, otherwise it won't work.

Once it's in, the new heart may still be rejected by the new body. How ungrateful! There are drugs that can help the new heart make friends with the body, but they can also make it more likely for the patient to get other diseases. Most heart transplants are very successful nowadays.

HANG ON, I HAVEN'T FINISHED WITH THAT YET!

Bet you never knew!

French doctor Francois-Joseph-Victor Broussais (1772-1838) thought leeches were lovely. He inspired French doctors to use more than 41 million slimy bloodsuckers a year. The potty physician used to plop the leeches on his cringing patients 50 at a time!

CONFUSING TRANSFUSION

Here's the blood-curdling story of blood transfusions. These medical miracles involve topping up someone's blood with more of the red stuff or replacing the whole lot with a fresh batch. Red-y, steady, blood flow!

...BY DRINKING IT?

TO MY HEALTH! HA HA HAAR!

NO WAY, JOSE!

BRAIN FOR WREN-T

IN THE 1660S, CHRISTOPHER WREN - ASTRONOMER, MATHS GENIUS, DOCTOR AND BRILLIANT BRAIN BEHIND ST PAUL'S CATHEDRAL - HAD A BETTER IDEA...

WREN MADE A SYRINGE OUT OF A GOOSE'S QUILL AND A PIG'S BLADDER AND TRIED TO INJECT A DOG...

I'M OUT OF HERE!

...WITH WINE!

MAYBE ISH NOT SCHO BAD... HIC!

IT WASN'T LONG BEFORE SOMEONE TRIED TO TRANSFER THE BLOOD OF ONE ANIMAL INTO ANOTHER. IN 1666, 'THE ROYAL SOCIETY' OF LONDON CARRIED OUT THE FIRST BLOOD TRANSFUSIONS - ON DOGS.

OK, I'M DEFINITELY OUTTA HERE!

THESE EARLY EXPERIMENTERS REMOVED A SMALL AMOUNT OF BLOOD FROM ONE DOG AND INJECTED IT INTO A SECOND DOG. THEY DRAINED AN EQUAL AMOUNT OF BLOOD FROM THE SECOND DOG BEFOREHAND - SO THE NEW BLOOD COULD 'FIT' IN.

THIS WON'T BE IN VEIN!

IT SURE FEELS LIKE IT!

IN FRANCE, DOCTORS WERE WORKING ON A SIMILAR IDEA. IN 1667, JEAN DENIS PUT LAMB'S BLOOD INTO A SICK BOY. THE BOY GOT BETTER BUT IT PROBABLY HAD NOTHING TO DO WITH HIS UNUSUAL REMEDY!

LOOK AT THE POOR LAMB

WHICH ONE?

ULP!

17

DENIS ALSO INJECTED ANOTHER PATIENT WITH CALF'S BLOOD. HE BELIEVED THAT AN INJECTION OF CALF'S BLOOD WOULD MAKE YOU AS GENTLE AS A LITTLE CALF.

YOU'LL FEEL AS GOOD AS MOO AFTER THIS

BUT THE PATIENT DIED, AND BLOOD TRANSFUSIONS BECAME UNPOPULAR FOR MANY YEARS AFTERWARDS.

WHAT ARE WE GOING TO DO WITH OUR PIGS' BLADDERS NOW?

IN 1818, JAMES BLUNDELL OF GUY'S HOSPITAL, LONDON, GOT THE BALL ROLLING AGAIN. HE CARRIED OUT THE FIRST HUMAN TO HUMAN BLOOD TRANSFUSION. IN 1840, HE AND SAMUEL LANE, GAVE A PATIENT A TOTAL BLOOD CHANGE.

OK, GUYS. GO WITH THE FLOW

BUT INJECTING PEOPLE WITH NEW BLOOD WAS STILL DANGEROUS AND WAS SOMETIMES FATAL.

AN AUSTRIAN, CALLED KARL LANDSTEINER, CAME TO THE RESCUE IN 1900. HE WAS A HARD-WORKING CHAP. VERY NICE. NOTHING PARTICULARLY ODD ABOUT HIM. OH ALL RIGHT, HE DID HANG A PLASTER CAST OF HIS DEAD MUM'S FACE ON THE WALL!

WELL AT LEAST I DIDN'T CHOP HER UP!

LANDSTEINER FOUND THAT HUMAN BLOOD IS DIVIDED INTO FOUR GROUPS - A, B, AB AND O.

I HOPE I GET AN 'A' FOR THIS TEST

THANKS TO HIS WORK, TRANSFUSIONS BECAME MUCH SAFER AS ONLY CERTAIN BLOOD TYPES MIX WITHOUT CLOTTING.

DURING THE FIRST WORLD WAR BLOOD TRANSFUSIONS WERE A LIQUID LIFE-SAVER. A CHEMICAL CALLED SODIUM CITRATE STOPPED BLOOD CLOTTING.

OH, YOU CLOT!

IT'S NO GOOD CRYING OVER SPILT BLOOD

AND LATER, IN THE 1920S, THE FIRST BLOOD BANKS OPENED THEIR DOORS.

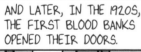

KINGS COLLEGE HOSPITAL LONDON

I'D LIKE TO MAKE A DEPOSIT

TOP YOUR TEACHER - THEY WEREN'T CALLED 'BLOOD BANKS' UNTIL DR BERNARD FANTUS COINED THE PHRASE IN 1937.

NOW TRANSFUSIONS ARE COMMON, BUT BLOOD BANKS STILL RELY ON DONORS - IT'S PAINLESS AND YOUR BODY SOON REPLACES THE BLOOD.

YEAH, AND IT'S BAGS OF FUN

THIS IS GREAT - YOU GET TO LIE DOWN ON THE JOB!

PUZZLES

I'M A MONSTER OF A PUZZLE!

Heart to Heart

This monster needs his blood cleaned. Follow his bloodstream all the way around his body starting and finishing at his heart, but make sure you go via the liver. Remember you can't make any U-turns!

BEING A LEECH, I'M A REAL SUCKER FOR BLOOD! I LOVE STEALING OTHER PEOPLE'S, EVEN THOUGH I'VE GOT MY OWN SUPPLY!

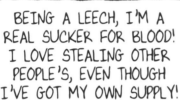

BLOOD TEST

Have a go at this blood-curdling quiz. Collect the letters from the correct answers, keep them in order, and at the end find out how many teeth a leech has.

1. What are the four main blood types?
a) A, B, AB and O   T
b) A, B, C and D   R   T
c) A, AX, AY, BZ   T

2. What did some devilish doctors use in the past to remove your blood if you were ill?
a) A vacuum cleaner   S
b) Leeches   S   H
c) X-rays   I

3. Which of these animals doesn't have any blood?
a) Dog   H
b) Jellyfish   R
c) Crocodile   R   P

4. What part of your blood sticks together to form scabs?
a) Red blood cells   F
b) White blood cells   F   K
c) Platelets   E

5. What stops your blood from travelling the wrong way round your blood vessels?
a) Valves   E
b) Traffic lights   U
c) Your liver   V

WIBBLE WOBBLE

VILE VACUUM

It's dark, there's dust everywhere and the air is warm and stinky. The noise is deafening and the ground is crawling with spider-like creatures munching on flakes of human skin. No, you're not in a horror film – you're in an old-style vacuum cleaner bag!

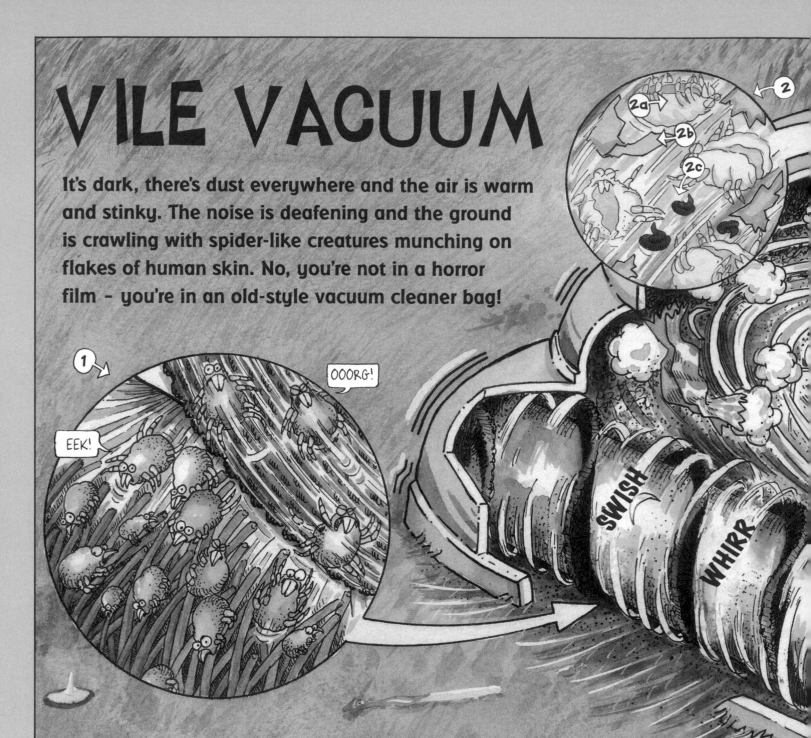

EEK!

OOORG!

SWISH

WHIRR

1. As the vacuum cleaner rolls over the carpet, it sucks up tiny mites that are hiding among the fibres. Adult mites are about 0.3 mm long and colourless – so you can't see them, which is just as well, as they are ugly little critters!

2. As well as mites, this vacuum cleaner sucks up ... hollow bodies of dead mites (**2a**), flakes of human skin (**2b**) and pellets of dust mite poo (**2c**)!

3. Vacuum cleaners such as this old one use a bag. The bag has to let air pass through it so it has a vent. A fine mesh or filter stops the dust and muck from just blowing out again. Trouble is mites' poo pellets are so tiny they can pass straight through. When someone cleans with this old dustbag, they are spraying mite poo all over the place.

Yuck! This is bad news since dust–mite poo can cause allergic reactions in some people.

4. A dark warmth of the cleaner bag is dust–mite heaven. When they're not scoffing all the food on offer, such as human skin flakes (yummy), dust mites are busy producing loads of baby dust mites!

5. There are also bogeys, toenails, sweet wrappers, pieces of sweetcorn, and other bits of food and grit in here.

6. Sometimes your carpet can attract some really rotten residents, such as fleas (**6a**) and carpet beetles (**6b**). Carpet beetle young are called 'woolly bears' but don't be fooled by the cute name – they grow into carpet–chomping adults.

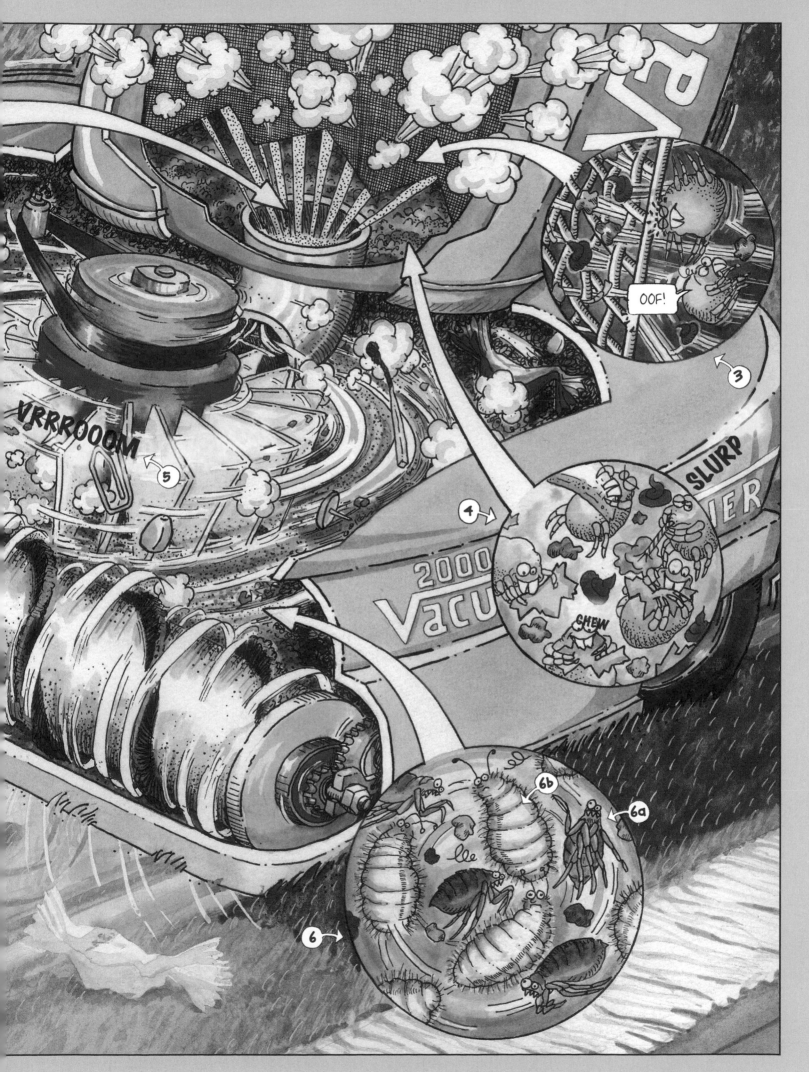

MANKY MICRO MITES

Slowly but surely, something's taking over the world. It's happening right under your nose, but you 'mite' not have noticed it. Everywhere you look you'll find them, but you've gotta look hard…

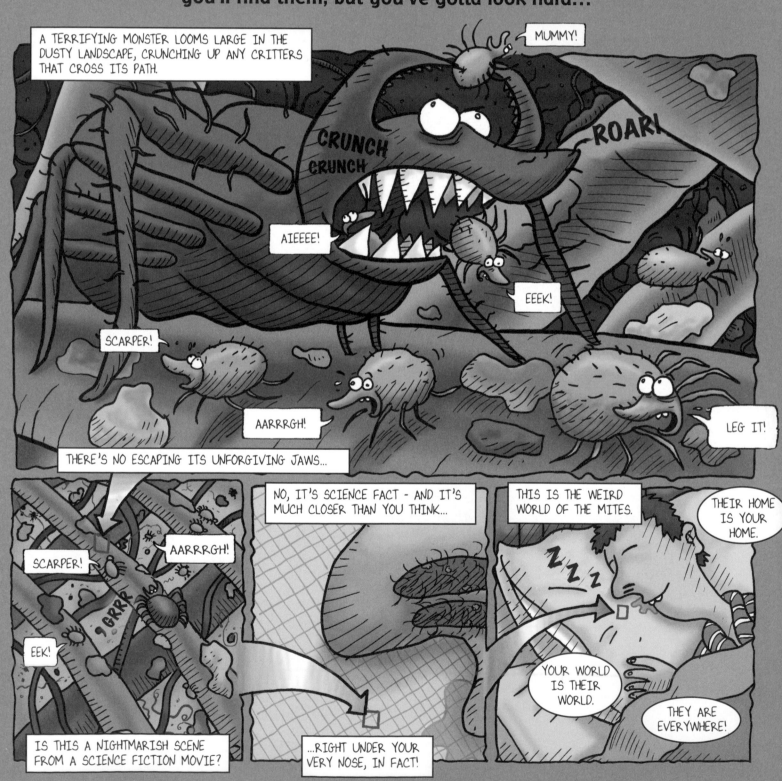

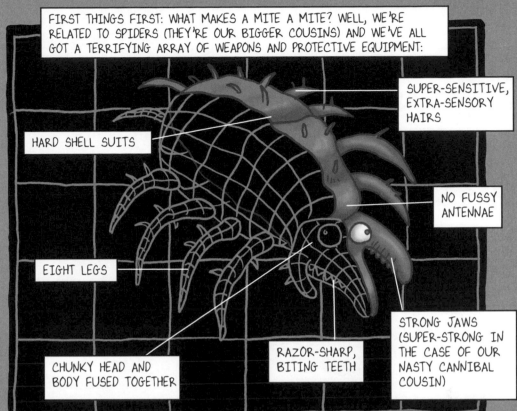

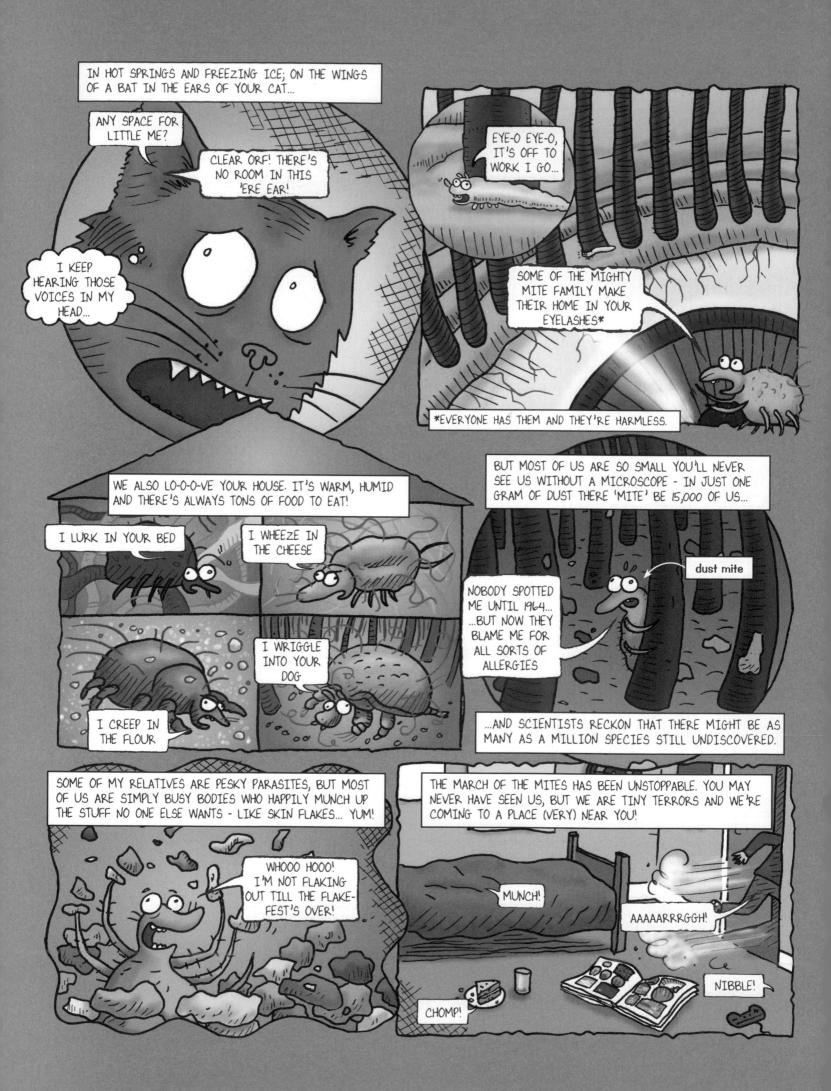

24

LOUSY LICE AND NUTTY NITS

Feeling itchy? That's probably because this dusty page has some lousy leftovers – and a head-scratching parasite test!

Home Swede Home

In one Swedish town in the Middle Ages a louse chose the mayor. The candidates laid their beards on a table in front of a louse. The owner of the beard chosen by the louse to live in was declared the mayor.

HIS ELECTIONS COMPLETELY LOUSY!

YEAH TOTALLY NITS!

A Lousy Experiment

Kooky but cool scientist Robert Hooke did loads of revolting experiments with blood-sucking bugs. One time, he took a body louse and let it bite him. Through his microscope he watched it sucking blood from his hand into its see-through body. He said:

I COULD PLAINLY SEE A SMALL CURRENT OF BLOOD WHICH CAME FROM ITS SNOUT AND POURED DIRECTLY INTO ITS BELLY

MITE-ILY TRUE OR FLEA-FULLY FALSE?

Here are some fascinating facts but with a few lousy lies thrown in. Do you reckon you can sniff out the true from the false ones?

1. Dust mites love drinking water. TRUE/FALSE

SLURP SLURP

2. Human fleas are amazing jumpers. If humans had the springing power of a flea we could jump over St Paul's Cathedral. TRUE/FALSE

3. Head lice are more likely to be found in dirty hair. TRUE/FALSE

4. Cat fleas are smaller than dog fleas. TRUE/FALSE

5. Your eyelashes have their own 'mite-y' cleaning service. TRUE/FALSE

6. The eggs of head lice are called nets. TRUE/FALSE

Answers on page 60

MONSTER MALARIA

Not all parasites creep and crawl. The world's deadliest parasite hangs out in mosquitoes' guts ... and inside peoples' blood cells!
So don't sweat it ... swat it!

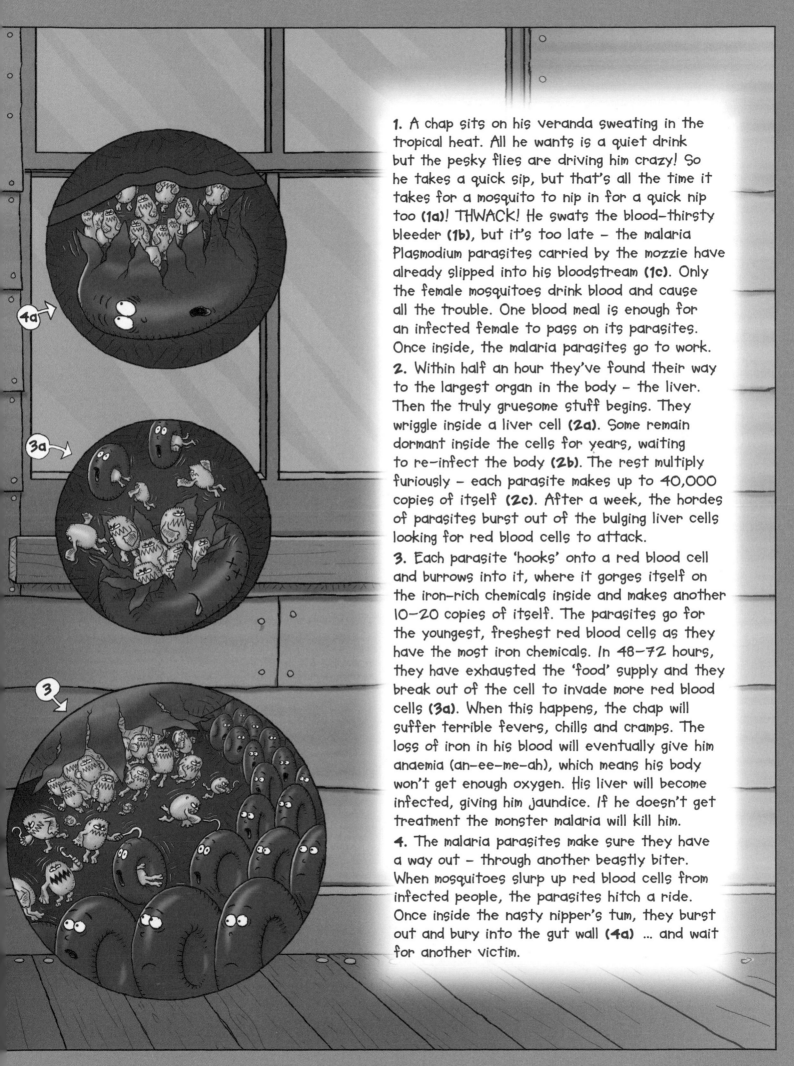

1. A chap sits on his veranda sweating in the tropical heat. All he wants is a quiet drink but the pesky flies are driving him crazy! So he takes a quick sip, but that's all the time it takes for a mosquito to nip in for a quick nip too **(1a)**! THWACK! He swats the blood-thirsty bleeder **(1b)**, but it's too late – the malaria Plasmodium parasites carried by the mozzie have already slipped into his bloodstream **(1c)**. Only the female mosquitoes drink blood and cause all the trouble. One blood meal is enough for an infected female to pass on its parasites. Once inside, the malaria parasites go to work.

2. Within half an hour they've found their way to the largest organ in the body – the liver. Then the truly gruesome stuff begins. They wriggle inside a liver cell **(2a)**. Some remain dormant inside the cells for years, waiting to re-infect the body **(2b)**. The rest multiply furiously – each parasite makes up to 40,000 copies of itself **(2c)**. After a week, the hordes of parasites burst out of the bulging liver cells looking for red blood cells to attack.

3. Each parasite 'hooks' onto a red blood cell and burrows into it, where it gorges itself on the iron-rich chemicals inside and makes another 10–20 copies of itself. The parasites go for the youngest, freshest red blood cells as they have the most iron chemicals. In 48–72 hours, they have exhausted the 'food' supply and they break out of the cell to invade more red blood cells **(3a)**. When this happens, the chap will suffer terrible fevers, chills and cramps. The loss of iron in his blood will eventually give him anaemia (an-ee-me-ah), which means his body won't get enough oxygen. His liver will become infected, giving him jaundice. If he doesn't get treatment the monster malaria will kill him.

4. The malaria parasites make sure they have a way out – through another beastly biter. When mosquitoes slurp up red blood cells from infected people, the parasites hitch a ride. Once inside the nasty nipper's tum, they burst out and bury into the gut wall **(4a)** ... and wait for another victim.

HORRID HUMANS

Ever wondered how we became the amazing animals that we are today? Well, here's the human race's evolution - and it's more like a mad assault course than a race, from monkeying around to mooching by the telly!

1. More than 5 million years ago (mya), human ancestors split away from the evolutionary 'branches' that would lead to today's great apes: the gorillas (1a), orang-utans (1b) and chimpanzees (1c). Time for our lot to get out of the jungle and take a different evolutionary course!

2. The race really began about 3-4 mya when an ape-like creature walked upright. Australopithecus afarensis still scoffed fruit nuts and leaves, but it could stand upright - which meant which it could move faster and see predators a lot sooner.

3. Farther along, about 3-2.4 mya, African Southern Ape (A. africanus) was a rather better walker. He was still on much the same diet, but was a bit smarter and even better at fighting and frightening off vicious wild doggy predators (3a).

4. Slightly later, at 2.7-1.4 mya, Nutcracker Man was bigger, tougher and bolder. Some think he had learned to use tools and could use a club to fight a sabre tooth tigers (4a).

5. Smarter still was Handy Man (Homo habilis) (2.6-1.4 mya). Mr Handy had developed a bigger brain and survived well. He was better with tools, using flint to chop down vines and slice up dead animals.

6. At the same level, but trying another route, was Work Man, Homo ergaster (2.0-1 mya). He was a bit bigger and used a spear.

7. Homo erectus (1.8–0.3 mya) was more upright and had the hot idea of fire! Great for fighting off wolves and cooking. He also made a basic hand-axe – good for hunting and fighting.

8. One type of Homo erectus (or maybe Homo heidelbergensis) was heading towards modern humans. They used stone-tipped spears, axes, wore furs, and looked a bit like modern humans.

9. Slightly farther ahead, but taking another route, was Neanderthal Man (190,000–28,000 ya). He was bigger, tougher and the best hunter around, even taking on huge woolly mammoths (9a). But he had a tough, cold life, and when the food ran out he didn't make it!

10. Homo sapiens (beginning 200,000 years ago) is basically modern man ... and has made it! He's hunting well, clambering through a cave, and has time to paint the walls with some art. He's well on his way to modern life!

11. And that's how we evolved into the only animal that can watch TV while eating crisps and parping at the same time. Evolution is brilliant!

EYE-POPPING INVENTIONS

Evolution has shaped and changed all the animals and plants on the Earth. Each step can take millions of years, but give it enough time and some amazing changes occur - for example, fish once grew feet*!

AMAZING EVOLUTION FACT FILE

NAME: Evolution

THE BASIC FACTS: Charles Darwin's Theory of Evolution, which took him 20 years to develop, explains that plants and animals change form over millions of years as they battle to survive. Here's how it works:

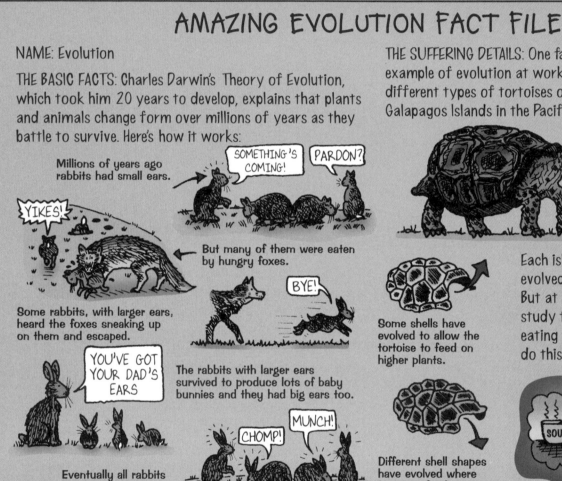

Millions of years ago rabbits had small ears.

SOMETHING'S COMING!

PARDON?

YIKES!

But many of them were eaten by hungry foxes.

Some rabbits, with larger ears, heard the foxes sneaking up on them and escaped.

BYE!

YOU'VE GOT YOUR DAD'S EARS

The rabbits with larger ears survived to produce lots of baby bunnies and they had big ears too.

Eventually all rabbits had big ears.

CHOMP!

MUNCH!

THE SUFFERING DETAILS: One famous example of evolution at work is the different types of tortoises of the Galapagos Islands in the Pacific.

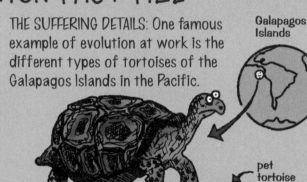

Galapagos Islands

pet tortoise

Some shells have evolved to allow the tortoise to feed on higher plants.

Different shell shapes have evolved where tortoises feed on ground-level plants.

Each island has a tortoise that evolved a slightly different shell. But at first Darwin didn't really study the tortoises. He enjoyed eating them in soup. Would you do this to your pet tortoise?

SOUP

D arwin's brilliant theory was based on research he did while sailing to the far reaches of the world on a ship called HMS *Beagle*. The differences he observed between similar species of plants and animals on the Galapagos Islands convinced Darwin that all modern lifeforms had evolved from ancient ancestors. That meant you could trace the origins of all living things on Earth back to slimy lifeforms that slithered in the primeaval soup of Earth's ancient seas. Which must have put him off his dinner a bit.

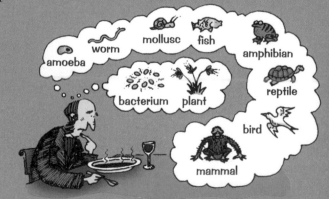

amoeba • worm • mollusc • fish • amphibian • bacterium • plant • reptile • bird • mammal

*Turn to page 36 for the whole fishy story!

Eyeball on the prize

It also explained how amazing organs developed - through small changes that take place over millions of years. For example, the goggling eyeballs you're using to read this page are the result of endless tiny tweaks since life began! Eyes started with a simple chemical that was sensitive to light. This was useful because it allowed its owner to tell whether it was:

• Out in the open, where it might be eaten by its enemies.

• Or under a stone, where it would be safe.

ARGH! WE NEED SOME OF THAT LIGHT-SENSITIVE STUFF!

PHEW!

Next, the light-detector chemical became concentrated in a light-sensitive patch inside a small pit in the skin, with just a tiny hole letting in light. The result was a kind of camera eye, which could form a basic picture. (Want to know how to make your own simple eye-like pinhole camera? You'll find out how on the next page.) The picture was clear enough to tell whether that animal lurking outside your home was a friend or an enemy.

From the pits

After that, eyes just got better and better, one step at a time. In some animals the pit became filled with jelly that bent the light rays and focused them on to light-sensitive cells. So the picture got clearer.

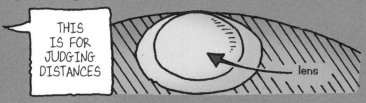

THIS IS FOR JUDGING DISTANCES

lens

Then the jelly hardened into a lens, which could be pulled by muscles into different shapes. This focused things that were close up or far away.

A layer of transparent skin then evolved to covered the delicate eye and protect it.

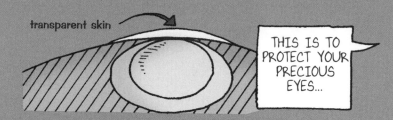

transparent skin

THIS IS TO PROTECT YOUR PRECIOUS EYES...

Then a pupil evolved inside the eye to open and close the hole where light entered. It could now work just as well in bright or dim light.

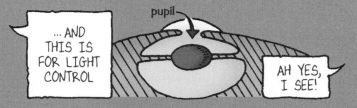

... AND THIS IS FOR LIGHT CONTROL

pupil

AH YES, I SEE!

It's taken evolution the best part of 1000 million years to come up with an eye like ours. And what's even more amazing is that it's done it more than once, in different groups of animals. Squid, which are members of the same family of animals as snails, have eyes that are almost as good as ours! And you never see squid wearing glasses, do you?

Bet you never knew!

Evolution doesn't just always go in one direction. Species can develop a feature, then, over millions of years, lose it again — because it's not needed. In many caves there are animals that never come outside. (These are called troglodytes. Your dad might call you it if you never get out of bed.) Some, such as the Texas blind salamander, evolved from ancestors that lived on the surface and had eyes. When they evolved into cave dwellers their eyes eventually disappeared — because they were useless in the darkness. The evolved an extra-sensitive sense of smell instead — much more useful in the total darkness. And it's happened to humans too. Yes, you have leftover bits of body parts that you've evolved not to need anymore. The knobbly bit at the bottom of your back — the coccyx — is where your ancestors had a tail. As far as evolution is concerned — either you use it or you lose it!

MAKE YOUR OWN PRIMITIVE EYE

Now you know that primitive animals could 'see' by using a 'camera eye' that formed a fuzzy but very useful picture. To help you see how these critters may have viewed their world, here's how to make your own pinhole camera.

You will need:
- a tube about 30cm long and 8cm wide
- aluminium foil
- sticky tape
- tracing paper or greaseproof baking paper
- a pin

HORRIBLE HEALTH WARNING!

WHEN YOU SEE THIS SYMBOL, ASK FOR HELP FROM AN ADULT.

1 Find a cardboard tube about 30 cm long and 8 cm wide – the exact size doesn't matter. The tubes used for posting rolled sheets of paper or calendars are ideal. You could make a tube by rolling a sheet of card and taping it lengthwise instead.

SHINE! CRINKLE!

2 Stretch a piece of aluminium foil over one end of the tube, bending it around the sides so that it's taut. Use sticky tape to secure the foil to the side of the tube.

TEE HEE

3 Over the other end of the tube, tape a piece of tracing paper (or greaseproof baking paper). Again, make sure it is stretched tight and flat.

POP!

4 Ask an adult to carefully prick the tiniest possible hole in the centre of the aluminium foil end using a sharp pin.

5 Point the pinhole at a bright window or bright light (but NEVER at the Sun). You'll see a faint image upside down on the tracing paper. This is how a pinhole camera works. Some animals, such as snails, have eyes like this.

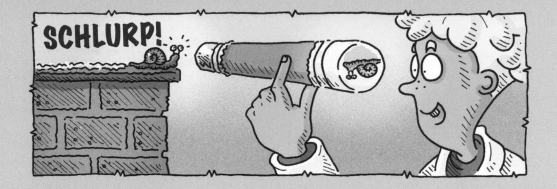
SCHLURP!

EERIE 3-D EYE EXPERIMENT

You will need:
- two A4 sheets of white card
- use of a photocopier
- scissors

1 Photocopy these two drawings of horrid school teacher Mrs Cross. Carefully cut out the two pictures.

A   B

2 Place picture A on top of one piece of white A4 card. Then take the other sheet of card and hold it on its side along the dotted line on picture A.

3 With your nose on the top edge of the card, look at the picture. Now relax your eyes as if looking into the distance.

4 Without moving your head, slide picture B into place on the right hand side of the card. Keep staring beyond the pictures.

SLIDE

5 The two pictures now blend together and you see a three-dimensional (3-D) image of Mrs Cross. Her face jumps out at you. This shows how animals that have evolved two eyes can see much more detail and depth than animals with primitive sight.

ELLIES' RELLIES

Human beings aren't the only brilliant animals with fascinating family trees. Here's the true tale of how elephants became the trumpeting wonders we know. It's a game of top trunks!

1. The family elephants developed from is called the Proboscidea – from 'proboscis' (pro-boss-iss) or trunk, which they've all had, some short, others long. About 50–60 million years ago (mya), elephant ancestors lived in extreme environments – from sweaty tropical rainforests to deserts.

2. One group of early hoofed mammals evolved into short-trunked creatures called Palaeomastodons, living around 30–34 mya. They were about 2 m tall. Their wallowing relatives Phosphatherium (**2a**) and Moeritherium (**2b**) didn't survive.

3. Primelephas led the way to our modern elephants. Stomping around 7–5 mya, it had powerful tusks and a longer trunk.

4. Branching off from Palaeomastodon, Gomphotherium was about 3.5 m tall with tusks in both the upper and lower jaw. It evolved into the Stegodon (**4a**), which may have been one of the mammoth's ancestors. Deinotherium (**4b**) was a goner, though.

5. The Trilopodon also evolved from a branch of Palaeomastodon's line, as did the stockier Mastodon (**5a**), which roamed Earth the same time as the mammoth.

6. The huge 3–4 m tall hairy mammoth, with its massive curly tusks, lived from 2 mya to 8000 years ago – and was hunted by early man. Quite a tusk! It seems to come from the same line as the modern Asian elephant (Elephas maximus) (**6a**). A separate branch from primelephas gave rise to the African bush elephant (Loxodonta africana) (**6b**) and the African forest elephant (L. cyclotis) (**6c**).

7. Related to both, cow-sized pygmy island elephants died out some 8000 years ago.

8. Still around today and distantly related to all these elephants are the curious underwater dugongs (sea cows) and manatees.

9. The hyrax is a surprising living rellie – tiny, trunkless and more like a rotten rodent!

SQUELCH!

SLOP!

SPLASH!

SPLOSH!

A FURRY TALE

Still a bit baffled about how evolution works? Well, who better than a lemur to explain the evolutionary leaps of mammals? From fish with fins then lungs and legs, it's a 'tail' that really goes up and down! Over to you then, Lee Moore…

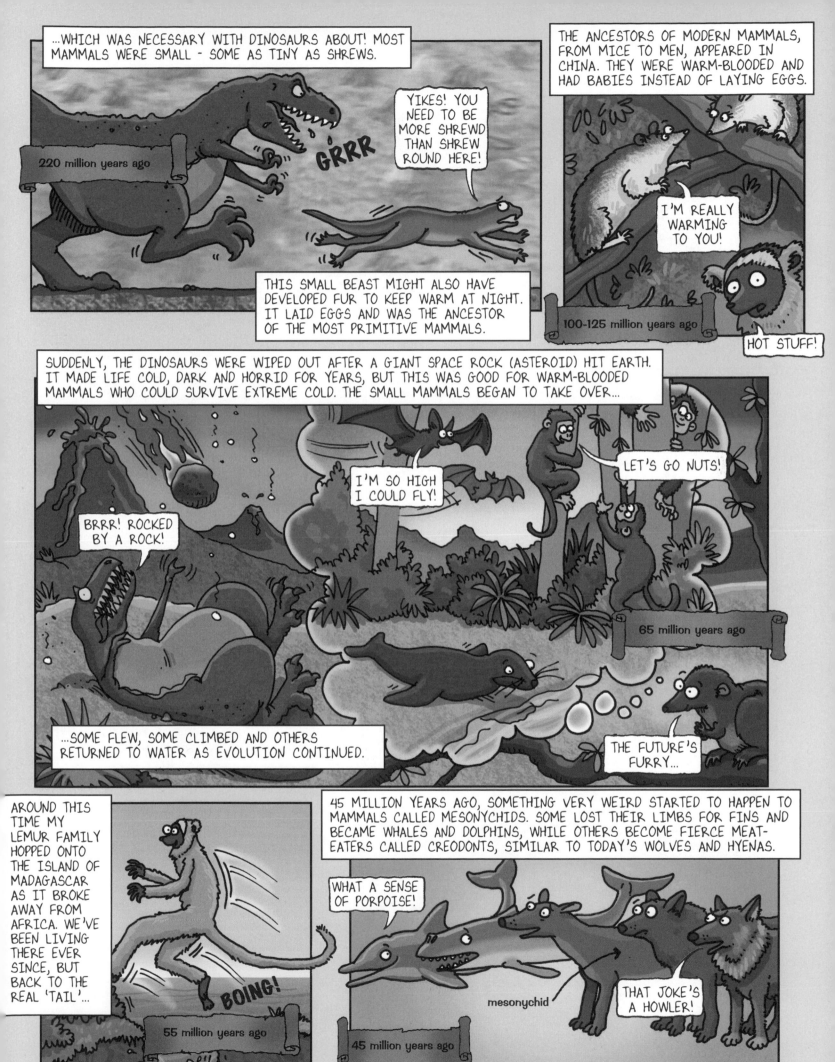

MEANWHILE, SOME MAMMALS - LIKE THESE TRUNKLESS EARLY ELEPHANTS - STAYED ON LAND.

HELLO! WHERE ARE OUR TRUNKS?

DUNNO. SHOULD WE MAKE A TRUNK CALL?

SPEOOSH!

CAN WE GO IN THE WATER WITHOUT TRUNKS?

40 million years ago

MAMMALS SPREAD FAR AND WIDE. THIS MONGOOSE TRAVELLED TO MADAGASCAR ACROSS THE SEA ON SOME FLOATING VEGETATION. HE BECAME THE ANCESTOR OF ALL THE MEAT-EATERS ON MY ISLAND!

YEAH, I'M SICK OF ALL THIS VEG!

21 million years ago

APES ALSO GOT EVERYWHERE. GIBBONS, ORANG-UTANS, GORILLAS AND CHIMPANZEES APPEARED. GUESS WHO'S THE SCARY MONKEY DOWN AT THE BOTTOM?

SWING WHEN YOU'RE WINNING!

WE'RE SO GREAT!

I'M ALWAYS HUNGRY

I'M GONNA BE THE BIG BOSS!

15 million years ago

THAT'S YOUR GREAT-GREAT-GREAT-GREAT-GRANDMA! READ THAT STORY IN ISSUE 33! HUMANS LIVED ON WHILE MAMMOTHS AND OTHER MASSIVE, HUNGRY MAMMALS DIED OUT...

...WHEN MAMMALS GET TOO BIG, THEY HAVE TROUBLE SUPPORTING THEIR OWN WEIGHT, THEY CAN'T RUN OR HIDE FROM STEALTHY PREDATORS AND THERE'S NOT ENOUGH FOOD FOR THEM.

SURVIVING IS A MAMMOTH TASK!

11 thousand years ago

IT'S TOO-TH HARD SOMETIMES!

TODAY, AT THE TOP OF THE MAMMAL TREE, HUMANS HAVE TAKEN CONTROL OF EARTH.

BURP!

Today!

I'M HIGHLY EVOLVED!

A MIGHTY ACHIEVEMENT!

PUZZLES

Terrible Timeline

If you were paying attention to the lemur's tale of mammal evolution, you'll have no trouble putting these events in order — from the beginning of Earth's history to the present day. Events within each upright column are in the correct order, but the columns themselves have been horribly jumbled up. The one farthest back in time has been done for you — column A=1. Now put 2, 3, 4, 5 and 6 in the correct boxes.

A 1   **B** ☐   **C** ☐   **D** ☐   **E** ☐   **F** ☐

Number Crunching Quiz

Start with the number 1037 and follow the maths instructions to find the ancient answers. Yes, ok, you can use a calculator!

1. If the whole story of life on Earth was written as a book and humans appeared in the last two lines of the last page, how many pages would the book have? (Take away 37.)

2. In the 1900s, people in the village of Zhoukoudian near Beijing in China found fossilized human bones. They ground them up and ate them in a medicine. How many years old were the bones? (Multiply by 200.)

3. In the past, the climate in Alaska was warmer and elephants, lions and camels lived there. How many years ago was this? (Take away 188,000)

Answers on page 60–61

MAD AS MATTER

Did you know that all matter in the universe, from solid and liquid to gas, is made of super-small particles? Follow the super-shrinking scientist Doctor Dot on a journey of discovery through time and tiny space to find out all about what matter's really made of – the awesome atom!

HAVING SHRUNK MYSELF TO A MICRODOT, I LEAPED INTO A TIME WORMHOLE TO BEGIN MY EPIC JOURNEY OF DISCOVERY. IT WAS A LITTLE ALARMING AT FIRST, BUT SOON I RATHER BEGAN TO ENJOY IT...

WEE-HEE!

I WENT BACK TO ANCIENT GREECE AROUND 460-370 BC, WHERE 'THE LAUGHING PHILOSOPHER' DEMOCRITUS BEGAN TO HAVE THE RIGHT IDEA ABOUT ATOMS. UNFORTUNATELY NO ONE ELSE BELIEVED HIM...

NUTTER!

HA HA HA! CUT A PIECE OF CHEESE IN HALF, THEN CUT AGAIN AND AGAIN. EVENTUALLY YOU'LL GET A PIECE TOO SMALL TO CUT IN HALF - THAT'S AN ATOM!

Dr Dot

SNIFF!

YIKES!

I HAD TO ESCAPE THAT RAVENOUS RODENT, SO I ZOOMED FORWARD TO ENGLAND IN 1808 TO SEE JOHN DALTON SHOWING THAT ATOMS OF DIFFERENT ELEMENTS HAVE DIFFERENT WEIGHTS AND PROPERTIES. JOHN D WAS A VERY STRICT, SERIOUS AND SCARY PURITAN ... BUT WHY DIDN'T HE WEAR BLACK?

ELEMENTS

AWFUL CLOTHES. HE CAN'T BE RIGHT!

ATOMS OF ELEMENTS COMBINE IN SIMPLE NUMBERS. DON'T ARGUE! I'M RIGHT!

Oxygen

Ammonia model

BIG HEAD!

Dr Dot

Hydro

OOPS! I'M UPSETTING THE THEORY!

POOR JOHN WAS COLOUR-BLIND AND WORE GHASTLY GARISH CLOTHES. THAT CAN'T HAVE HELPED HIM, BUT HE WAS RIGHT...

THAT AMMONIA IDEA STINKS!

...UNFORTUNATELY FEW BELIEVED HIM...

...WHERE THE GERMAN SCIENTIST FRIEDRICH KEKULÉ WAS SNOOZING ON A LONDON BUS. HE WAS ABOUT TO HAVE A VERY IMPORTANT DREAM...

DALTON HAD MADE SOME GREAT DISCOVERIES, SO I WENT ON TO 1854...

...HIS HEAD FILLED WITH DANCING ATOMS...

WHEN HE WOKE UP, HE HAD A NIFTY IDEA ABOUT HOW ATOMS JOIN TOGETHER TO MAKE MOLECULES, AND BEGAN TO BUILD MODELS TO FIND OUT THEIR STRUCTURE - OF COURSE I COULD HAVE TOLD HIM!

CAN I HELP?

NINE YEARS LATER, KEKULÉ WAS SUFFERING FROM 'FLU AND WORRYING ABOUT MOLECULAR FORMATION IN BENZENE, A CHEMICAL IN COAL. HE WASN'T THE ONLY ONE SUFFERING...

A-CHOO!

Dr Dot

URRGH! GROSS!

PSSSSSST! FREDDY! WAKE UP! KETTLE'S BOILING!

KEKULÉ FELL INTO A FEVERISH SLEEP... AND FOR SOME REASON STARTED TO DREAM OF SNAKES...

PSSST!

PSSST!

PSSST!

IN HIS DREAM, A SNAKE BITES ITS OWN TAIL, AND THIS INSPIRED KEKULÉ TO PICTURE THE 12-ATOM STRUCTURE OF BENZENE, AND GREATLY HELPED US UNDERSTAND HOW ATOMS ORDER THEMSELVES...

THEN AGAIN, UNFORTUNATELY NOT EVERYONE BELIEVED IT...

BUT BENZENE IS RING-SHAPED!

DREAM ON!

GET ATOM!

YOU SNAKE IN THE GRASS!

NOW TO 1897, WHERE CAMBRIDGE SCIENTIST JJ THOMPSON WAS DISCOVERING THAT THERE WERE EVEN SMALLER ELECTRO-MAGNETICALLY CHARGED PARTICLES INSIDE ATOMS, KNOWN AS ELECTRONS. FELLOW SCIENTIST LORD KELVIN WAS EATING A PUDDING, SO THIS GAVE HIM AN IDEA OF WHAT TO CALL IT...

THIS REALLY BECAME THE 'PLUM PUDDING MODEL', WHERE LIKE RAISINS, NEGATIVELY CHARGED ELECTRONS WERE SEEN AS EVENLY SPREAD IN A PUDDING-LIKE ATOM THAT HAD A POSITIVE ELECTROMAGNETIC CHARGE.

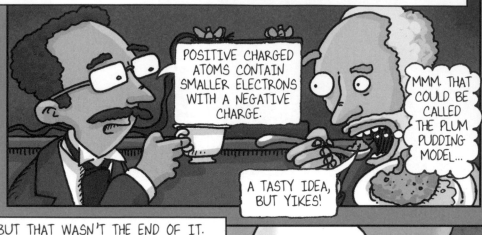

POSITIVE CHARGED ATOMS CONTAIN SMALLER ELECTRONS WITH A NEGATIVE CHARGE.

MMM. THAT COULD BE CALLED THE PLUM PUDDING MODEL...

A TASTY IDEA, BUT YIKES!

PHEW! HERE'S RAISINS TO BE CHEERFUL!

BUT THAT WASN'T THE END OF IT. MAKING MYSELF EVEN SMALLER, I FIZZLED OVER TO KIWI SCIENTIST ERNEST RUTHERFORD IN 1910, AND GOT CAUGHT UP IN HIM SHOOTING TINY ALPHA PARTICLES AT SOME VERY THIN GOLD FOIL...

WEE-HEE! WE SHOULD PASS RIGHT THROUGH THIS!

BUT MUCH TO OUR SURPRISE, SOME PARTICLES REBOUNDED RIGHT BACK. THIS MEANT THAT THE STRUCTURE OF GOLD ATOMS WAS UNEVEN - THERE WERE GAPS TO PASS THROUGH, BUT ALSO A SOLID PART WE BOUNCED OFF, CALLED THE NUCLEUS.

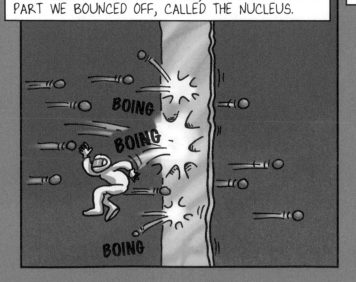

BOING
BOING
BOING

IT WAS A CRAZY, COMPLICATED FLIGHT, BUT BY THE WAY PARTICLES REBOUNDED, RUTHERFORD ESTABLISHED THAT AN ATOM HAS A TINY NUCLEUS IN THE MIDDLE WITH SMALLER ELECTRONS WHIZZING AROUND IT, LIKE MOONS ROUND A PLANET!

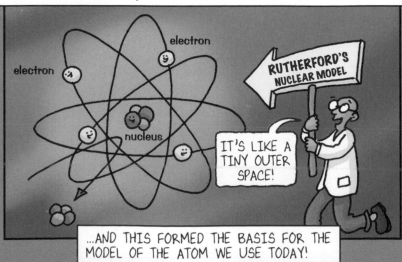

electron
electron
nucleus

RUTHERFORD'S NUCLEAR MODEL

IT'S LIKE A TINY OUTER SPACE!

...AND THIS FORMED THE BASIS FOR THE MODEL OF THE ATOM WE USE TODAY!

ATOMS' POTTY PATTERNS

Tea cups crack if you bash 'em and ice cubes crunch then melt when you gnash 'em. But why? What is it that makes hard stuff tough, slippy stuff sloppy – and why is water so wetly weird?

Have you ever wondered why some solid objects are bendy and others are tough? No? Well, have you ever pondered why your auntie's best china is always breaking and why her rock cakes are … erm, as hard as rock? Well, here's why:

• In every solid object the atoms are bonded together. But what matters is the way the atoms are arranged.

• If they're in stretchy strings the object will be stretchy like an elastic band. This means you can squash them together quite easily.

• In very hard materials such as diamonds the atoms are arranged in a very tight and strong framework.

• In softer materials such as graphite – which is used to make pencil lead – the atoms are arranged in loose layers that rub off easily when you write.

• In china the atoms are closely packed and joined tightly together. But if just one atomic join breaks, the china will crack.

• In a metal the atoms are surrounded by a crowd of jostling electrons. (They're a bit like teachers in a playground at break-time.) The electrical force of the electrons keeps the atoms in place. But each atom can move a bit and that's why you can bend metal – if you're very strong!

Melting Moments
Here are five mad facts about water molecules:

1. Snow and hail form when water molecules join up and freeze in the sky. Hailstones are made when lumps of ice swirl around in a cold cloud getting larger and larger. The largest hailstone was the size of a football.

2. In very cold places from northern Canada to Siberia some lakes freeze solid. The freezing starts with a single ice-crystal that grows and grows. So, by the end, each frozen lake has become one giant ice-crystal.

3. As water freezes it expands and crushes anything it traps with a force of 140 kg per square cm … enough to sink a ship or crush a man to death.

4. You can make snowballs because snow is partly melted ice, which can be squished. In the Antarctic, the snow is too hard and powdery for snowball fights.

5. As ice melts the molecules take in heat energy and wobble. Finally, they wobble free and float around.

wobbling molecule ← melting ice cube

POSH 'N' PARPY MATTER PARTY

From precious stones to heavy metals, leakings of liquid to gurgling gases, welcome to the Mad as Matter Masked Party, where solids, liquids and gases are on the move!

1. The boys are letting off stink-bomb gas made from liquid ammonia mixed with sulphur (from match heads). The result is foul-smelling ammonium sulphide. Pooh!

2. Almost as stinky – hydrogen sulphide, let off in awful farts – and someone's been doing a few... !

3. Champagne contains cheeky carbon-dioxide (CO_2) gas bubbles – that's a carbon atom joined to two oxygen atoms.

4. Sugar crystals of carbon, oxygen and hydrogen form a sweet-tasting, six-sided hexagonal shape.

5. The ice sculpture is melting back to its liquid form.

6. Pretty ruby atoms take the form a six-sided hexagonal shape.

7. The crystals of salt you put on food are sodium and chlorine atoms making sodium chloride cubes.

8. Diamonds have a very strong structure. Each carbon atom is always joined to four others.

9. Gold is one of the purest and most prized metals.

10. The coins we use today aren't gold. 'Copper' coins are actually copper and tin, and the silver-coloured ones are made of nickel and copper.

11. Every crystallized snowflake, cooled quickly from water vapour high in the air, forms its own unique shape.

12. When it's cold outside, and a room gets really hot from a fire or people dancing and getting sweaty, clouds of steam form liquid condensation.

13. Party balloons contain helium. They float because helium is lighter than air. It's the second lightest gas after hydrogen. It can help dogs fly!

14. For a period, natural gas was used for heating and lighting, and it was usually safer than candles (14a)!

15. In the early twentieth century, the idea of electric current being carried through copper wire to power lights was a sparky new thing.

Find five pongy sulphide molecules parping loose round this picture!

45

CRYSTAL CAVE

Crystals are groups of atoms arranged in boxy shapes, fitted together in larger boxes of the same shape. Many great crystals are found underground. Let's dig a little bit deeper…

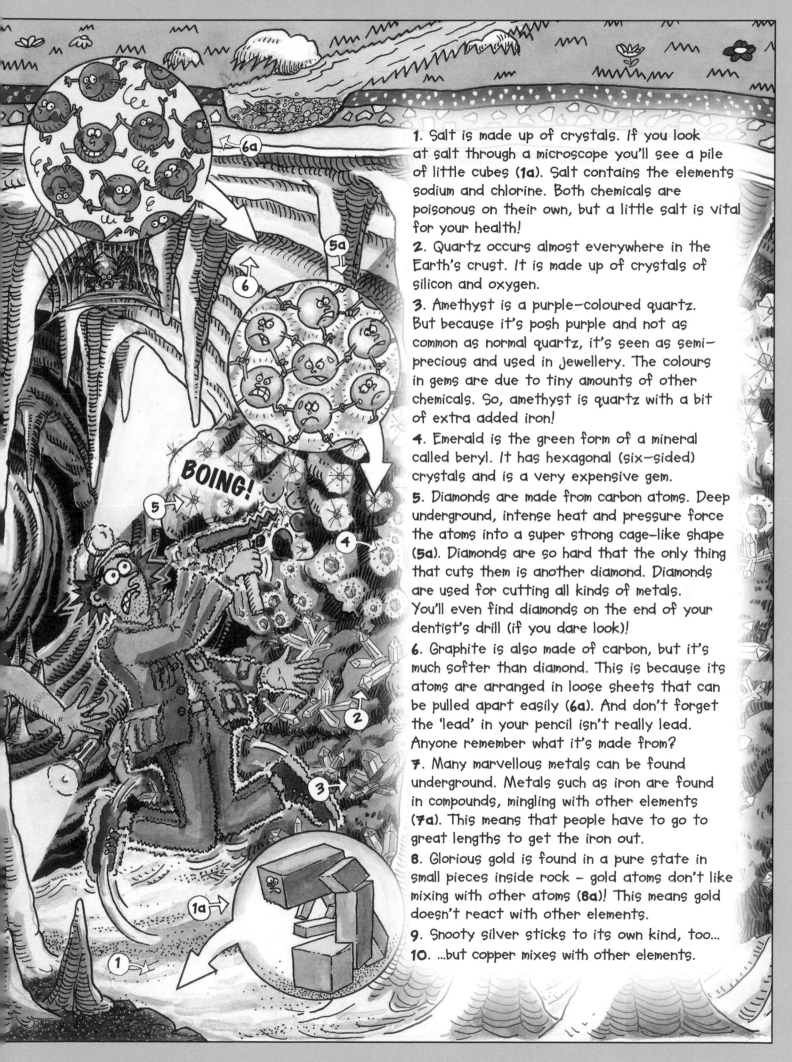

1. Salt is made up of crystals. If you look at salt through a microscope you'll see a pile of little cubes (**1a**). Salt contains the elements sodium and chlorine. Both chemicals are poisonous on their own, but a little salt is vital for your health!

2. Quartz occurs almost everywhere in the Earth's crust. It is made up of crystals of silicon and oxygen.

3. Amethyst is a purple-coloured quartz. But because it's posh purple and not as common as normal quartz, it's seen as semi-precious and used in jewellery. The colours in gems are due to tiny amounts of other chemicals. So, amethyst is quartz with a bit of extra added iron!

4. Emerald is the green form of a mineral called beryl. It has hexagonal (six-sided) crystals and is a very expensive gem.

5. Diamonds are made from carbon atoms. Deep underground, intense heat and pressure force the atoms into a super strong cage-like shape (**5a**). Diamonds are so hard that the only thing that cuts them is another diamond. Diamonds are used for cutting all kinds of metals. You'll even find diamonds on the end of your dentist's drill (if you dare look)!

6. Graphite is also made of carbon, but it's much softer than diamond. This is because its atoms are arranged in loose sheets that can be pulled apart easily (**6a**). And don't forget the 'lead' in your pencil isn't really lead. Anyone remember what it's made from?

7. Many marvellous metals can be found underground. Metals such as iron are found in compounds, mingling with other elements (**7a**). This means that people have to go to great lengths to get the iron out.

8. Glorious gold is found in a pure state in small pieces inside rock – gold atoms don't like mixing with other atoms (**8a**)! This means gold doesn't react with other elements.

9. Snooty silver sticks to its own kind, too...

10. ...but copper mixes with other elements.

HOW TO GET A BOILED EGG INTO A BOTTLE

Amaze your friends and family with this egg-citing trick. All it takes is hot air, a glass bottle, a boiled egg ... and the magic of science!

HORRIBLE HEALTH WARNING!

Don't do this experiment when you're hungry or you may accidentally eat the boiled egg. If this happens fill a balloon with water to the size of an egg, knot it, and use this instead. When you see this symbol, ask for help.

You will need:
- one small egg
- a glass juice bottle with a neck that is just a little too small for an egg to fit through ... about 3.5 cm (the bottle can't be plastic, or the trick won't work)
- hot tap water

1 Ask an adult to help you boil the egg. This trick works best if the egg is soft-boiled – about five minutes should do it.

2 Cool the egg in cold running water afterwards. Now the smelly bit ... remove the shell (carefully, so that you don't damage the egg or it could fall apart during the trick ... you don't want scrambled egg).

3 Take the lid off your glass bottle. Run the hot tap until it's as hot as you can bear without getting burned. Put the plug in the sink and fill it up with hot water. Now submerge your bottle. And leave it to warm up for about three minutes.

4 Remove the bottle from the sink and tip out the hot water. Now, place the boiled egg on the neck of the bottle (pointed end down).

SQUISH!

AIR MOLECULES

I'M SO EXCITED

I'M FEELING A BIT DEPRESSED

ME TOO!

5 Stand back and watch. Inside the bottle, the air molecules are rushing about excitedly at first, because they're hot. But as the bottle cools down, the air molecules cool too. They become less excited and move around less. This lowers the air pressure inside the bottle so that it is less than the air pressure outside the bottle. And so the egg gets sucked in.

PLOP!

6 Plop! And in it goes... your very own egg in a bottle. If you keep the science behind this trick a secret, you'll amaze your friends and family. They'll never guess how you did it. (Unless they're *Horrible Science* fans too!)

HORRIBLE HEALTH WARNING!

Don't be impatient ... it can take up to 10 minutes for the egg to be 'sucked' into the bottle. Don't be tempted to mash it in with your fist ... the point of the trick is to get a whole egg into the bottle WITHOUT touching it.

Top ship

You've heard of a ship in a bottle? Well this is an egg in a bottle. If you learn how to do them both, you'll end up with eggs and ships in a bottle. Mmmm! (Sounds tasty but it's actually just a bad joke.)

Confusing Chemicals

Lots of things you find around the house have confusing chemical names. Super for scientists, but completely confusing for the rest of us. Can you guess what these show-offs are talking about?

CAN YOU PASS THE SODIUM CHLORIDE, PLEASE?

NOW, WHERE DID I LEAVE MY MAGNESIUM SILICATE?

WHEN I WAS A BOY WE USED TO WRITE WITH CALCIUM CARBONATE

DO YOU WANT ACETIC ACID ON THEM?

Answers on page 61

MUM MACHINE

It's an ordinary school day, but mum's not feeling too well … so she pulls a lever and unleashes the monster super-mum machine instead. Watch out, kids!

1. Mum uses the first simple machine – a lever **(1a)** – to release a ball. This rolls to the bedroom and knocks over a bucket of water **(1b)**, which pours out onto your head. Wakey wakey!

2. Pulleys and gears work rubber glove hands to slap the sleep out of you and a gear system turns the bed into a ramp that slides you down to the bathroom.

3. Gravity lands you with a splash in the bath. Another gear system works the scrubbing, cleaning machine. Pulleys and weights turn a wheel and axle **(3a)** to switch the shower from hot to cold. Brr! Get out!

4. A lever lifts a weight, activating another pulley and gear system that drops you into your school uniform **(4a)**. Careful the cat doesn't get dressed as well!

5. A 'dumb waiter' lift (operated by weights and pulleys) whizzes you down to the kitchen.

6. Gears attached to the windmill (wheel and axle) power the rest of the machine.

7. Pulleys and hooks lure you with chocolate and put you in front of a healthier breakfast. An egg-cracker acts as a wedge **(7a)**, a spring in the toaster makes toast pop up and pulleys bring more food **(7b)**. The rubber udder container sprays milk over your cereal **(7c)**.

8. Finally you're dragged by ropes and pulleys to the living room, where a piston 'loading device' sends school books down an inclined plane (ramp) **(8a)** into your satchel. Rubber lips on a wheel and crank system **(8b)** kiss you goodbye. Looks like dad's been got ready for school, too!

MANIC MACHINE-MAKERS

Machine-making maniacs have been bashing together bits of wood for centuries, but none as brilliant and bold as a gleeful Greek and an ingenious Italian, who were both a bit barmy!

IT'S 220BC IN SYRACUSE, AND ECCENTRIC GREEK GENIUS MATHEMATICIAN ARCHIMEDES HAS BEEN FORCED BY HIS SERVANTS TO TAKE A BATH, BECAUSE HE SMELLED SO BAD.

GRR! THIS IDEA STINKS

SO DO YOU, SIR

ANARCHIC ARCHIE LIKED TO DRAW DIAGRAMS ON HIS BODY AND SUDDENLY HAD SOME INSPIRATION...

LEAPING JOYFULLY OUT OF THE BATH, HE TOLD EVERYBODY...

EUREKA! EUREKA! I'VE FOUND IT!

OOH! HE'S GOT IT!

LOST IT MORE LIKE!

ARCHIMEDES HAD WORKED OUT THAT HIS OWN LOSS OF WEIGHT WHEN HE GOT IN THE BATH WAS EQUAL TO THE AMOUNT OF WATER SPILLED FROM THE BATH.

USING THIS METHOD, HE FOILED A CROOKED JEWELLER WHO HAD TRIED TO CON THE KING BY ADDING SILVER TO HIS NEW GOLD CROWN.

AHA! THERE'S MORE SILVER IN THIS CROWN

MY GUILT IS HEAVY

THAT'S A WEIGHT OFF MY MIND

ARCHIMEDES HAD WORKED OUT THAT A CROWN WITH SOME SILVER IN IT SPILLED LESS WATER THAN ONE WHICH ONLY CONTAINED THE HEAVIER METAL GOLD.

WHEN IT CAME TO MAKING MACHINES, THE WEIGHT OF OBJECTS WAS VERY IMPORTANT. ARCHIMEDES'S SCREW WAS A BRILLIANT DEVICE TO PUMP WATER FROM THE HOLD OF SHIPS.

NORMALLY I SWEAT BUCKETS

THAT'S THE WAY!

HOLD ONTO THAT IDEA!

THE SCREW, BEING TURNED AT 45 DEGREES AROUND A CYLINDER, TOOK THE HEAVY WATER OUT GRADUALLY AND FAR MORE EASILY THAN WITH BUCKETS.

ARCHIMEDES WAS A NUTTY GENIUS, BUT EVEN HE WAS BETTERED BY AN AMAZING 15TH CENTURY INVENTOR, WHO TOOK HIS IDEAS EVEN FURTHER - LEONARDO DA VINCI!

LEONARDO WAS OBSESSED WITH WATER. HE EVEN DEVISED A LEATHER DIVING SUIT AND A DIVING BELL. IN EARLY VERSIONS AIR WAS PUMPED DOWN TO THE DIVER FROM THE SHIP.

GEARS AND SCREWS HELP SUPPLY THE WATER...

WAT-ER DRINKER!

WAT-ER THINKER!

GUSH

GLUG!

GURGLE

SQUEAK

I COULD DO WITH A BREATHER

SO COULD I!

LEONARDO'S WATER LIFT USED TWO ARCHIMEDES SCREWS AND TWO TOWERS. CARRIED BY GRAVITY, THE WATER COULD RUN MILLS, BRING WATER SUPPLY TO HOUSES AND EVEN ALLOW FLUSHING TOILETS!

LEONARDO EVEN DESIGNED A CAR THAT MOVED ON ITS OWN BY SPRINGS AND GEARED WHEELS...

I'M DRIVEN BY MY IDEAS!

WHIRR   GRIND

...AGAIN NO ONE TOOK THIS IDEA FURTHER UNTIL BENZ AND DAIMLER BUILT CARS ABOUT 400 YEARS LATER!

BUT LATER LEO DESIGNED AIR TANKS, SO THE DIVER COULD BE FREE OF AIR PUMPS. THIS INVENTION WAS NOT PROPERLY USED BY DIVERS UNTIL THE 20TH CENTURY. IT WAS BREATHTAKING!

LEONARDO WAS BRILLIANT AT MATHS AND ARCHITECTURE, AND HE ALSO CREATED GREAT PAINTINGS, INCLUDING HIS FAMOUS 'MONA LISA'. THIS SKILL REALLY HELPED HIM DEVISE HIS INVENTIONS WITH PRECISE DRAWINGS...

LEONARDO OFTEN HAD HIS HEAD IN THE CLOUDS AND LEFT MANY IDEAS UNFINISHED. BUT HE UNDERSTOOD WEIGHT, THE PRINCIPLES OF FLIGHT, DESIGNED A PARACHUTE AND EVEN A ROTATING AIRSCREW HELICOPTER!

FLAP FLAP

HE'S A BIRD BRAIN!

THIS IDEA'S SCREWY!

GERONIMO!!!

NO ONE KNOWS IF LEONARDO BUILT FROM HIS PLANS. THEY MAY HAVE BEEN TOO DANGEROUS, BUT THEY WERE WELL AHEAD OF THEIR TIME.

AREN'T YOU PAINTING ME?

LATER, LISA - DON'T BE SUCH A MONA!

HE ALSO LOVED ANIMALS, AND EVEN DRESSED HIS PET LIZARD AS A DRAGON TO SCARE PEOPLE OFF WHEN HE WAS BUSY!

...BUT HOW DID LOONY LEONARDO GET MONEY FOR ALL THIS? HE COULDN'T PAY HIS WAY AS A PAINTER, SO HE HAD TO BE EMPLOYED BY SOME POWERFUL AND SCARY FIGURES.

I LOVE WAR!

Duke of Milan – employed Leo until 1499 when the French invaded.

D'YA GET THE POINT!?

Cesare Borgia – son of the Pope, loved to stab people in the back.

DON'T MESS WITH ME!

King Francis I – French king who liked expensive gifts.

LEONARDO HATED WAR, BUT HAD TO DESIGN MANY AMAZING WAR MACHINES FOR HIS PATRONS. THESE INCLUDED A TANK POWERED BY MEN TURNING CRANKS AND PULLEYS...

PULL-EY THE OTHER ONE!

TWANG RUMBLE

DON'T GET SO CRANKY!

...A MONSTER MACHINE GUN WITH 33 GUNS AND A CRAZY CROSSBOW POWERED BY MEN WALKING ON A WHEEL...

THIS MUST HAVE COST A BOMB!

EXCELLENT!

YEAH, THE DUKE MUST BE LOADED

...BUT MOST AMAZINGLY, TO WELCOME THE FRENCH KING, A SUIT OF ARMOUR THAT MOVED ON ITS OWN AND A WALKING MECHANICAL LION THAT SPROUTED FLOWERS FROM ITS CHEST!

HURRAY! HURRAY! HURRAY!

CREAK

PING

IT'S LEO THE LION!

LEONARDO CREATED MANY HUNDREDS OF OTHER MACHINES BY COMBINING SIMPLE MACHINES LIKE WEIGHTS AND PULLEYS, MANY NOT PROPERLY DEVELOPED FOR MORE THAN 400 YEARS. HE REALLY WAS AHEAD OF HIS TIME!

I HOPE IT WAS WORTH THE 'WEIGHT'!

PUZZLES

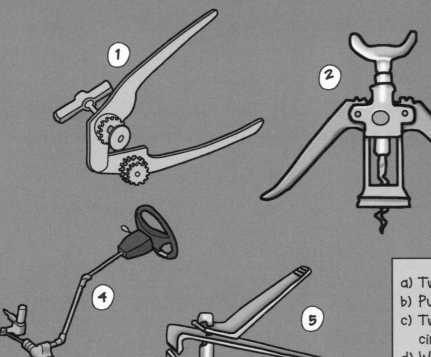
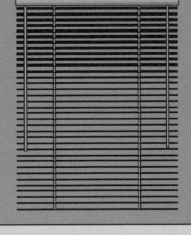

Machine Match-up
Match the marvellous everyday machines to the combinations of simple machine parts they use.

a) Two levers and two wedges
b) Pulleys
c) Two levers, wheel & axle, three gear cogs, circular wedge
d) Wheel & axle, rack & pinion gears and angled joints
e) Two levers, rack & pinion gears and screw

Pedal-powered Products
The bicycle was such a good idea that 19th-century inventors began to peddle their own machines. Which of these are too silly to be true?

1. IDEAL FOR SHIPWRECKS
Amaze your friends and escape the sharks! The pedal-powered life preserver.

sail – useful if you tire of pedalling

comfy air-filled rubber ring

propellers

lamp for SOS signals

2. GET YOUR NAME IN WRITING
With our tricycle-powered printing press!

ink tank

solid rubber letters on tyres

3. DON'T MISS OUR BUS!
No more school bus breakdowns. Try the new pedal-powered school bus. Special pedals under the seats linked to a rotating crankshaft power the bus at 22 mph.

Pedal Power!

Answers on page 61

ENERGETIC ENGINES

So now you know all about simple machines, but what about the clanking, clanging complicated machines we see all around us, like cars? The facts will get you revved up, but may drive you round the bend!

All machines, from tin openers to tanks, are cunning combinations of simple machines. As in the monstrous mum-machine, each gear and pulley does its own little job, but when they're put together they do some crazily complex stuff. A car is a box that contains hundreds of little machines each doing one job.

Whatever the task – from striking a note on a piano to grinding up the ground – the idea is to make life a little easier by saving us energy. For example, using a tin opener uses less energy than the alternative…

Power gobblers

Some machines – 'energetic engines' – need a lot more power than any human can provide. Energetic engines are at the heart of almost

I KNOW WHAT I PREFER!

every contraption we use today, but it wasn't long ago that horses and water-powered wheels did the hard work. Then along came steam power – and that changed everything. (The geeky Greeks knew all about steam power, but they seemed to prefer using slaves!)

Sizzling steam

It took another 1,600 years for a hot-head called Thomas Savery to re-invent the idea. His first design was used to pump water out of mines, but the engine was unreliable and prone to going BANG!

The steam engine was worked on and improved, and was soon miles better than Savery's simple steam-dream. James Watt was the top inventor of his day and his engine blew everyone else's away – without blowing up.

WATT STEAM ENGINE

3. Piston passes movement energy to wheel.

4. Drive belt transfers movement energy to machinery.

WHAT'S THIS MACHINE, WATT?

THIS IS WHAT I CALL MY WATT STEAM ENGINE

WHAT D'YOU MEAN WATT, WATT?

WHAT? WHAT WATT?

2. Heat energy boils water to steam – steam has movement energy.

1. Energy stored in the form of coal – coal burned to make heat energy.

Crazy Car Contraptions

A modern car is little more than a metal box crammed with machines that do simple tasks. Things like a lever pedal that pulls a cord that lets a bit more fuel into the engine (accelerator); or an electrically operated gear system that raises and lowers a pane of glass (electric windows). Each of these parts is a small machine made from different combinations of about eight simple machines. They all work smoothly together to get you from place to place (or not, in the case of your grandad's old banger)!

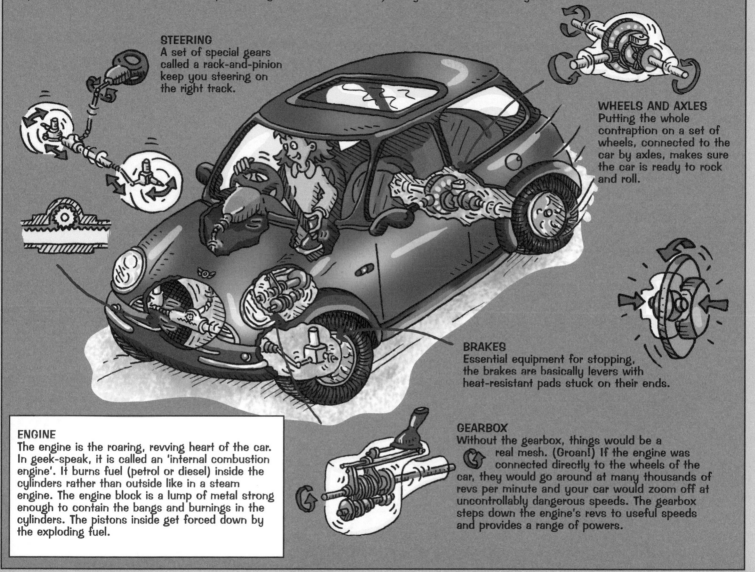

STEERING
A set of special gears called a rack-and-pinion keep you steering on the right track.

WHEELS AND AXLES
Putting the whole contraption on a set of wheels, connected to the car by axles, makes sure the car is ready to rock and roll.

BRAKES
Essential equipment for stopping, the brakes are basically levers with heat-resistant pads stuck on their ends.

ENGINE
The engine is the roaring, revving heart of the car. In geek-speak, it is called an 'internal combustion engine'. It burns fuel (petrol or diesel) inside the cylinders rather than outside like in a steam engine. The engine block is a lump of metal strong enough to contain the bangs and burnings in the cylinders. The pistons inside get forced down by the exploding fuel.

GEARBOX
Without the gearbox, things would be a real mesh. (Groan!) If the engine was connected directly to the wheels of the car, they would go around at many thousands of revs per minute and your car would zoom off at uncontrollably dangerous speeds. The gearbox steps down the engine's revs to useful speeds and provides a range of powers.

FOUR-STROKE CYCLE

The internal combustion engine works in four stages:

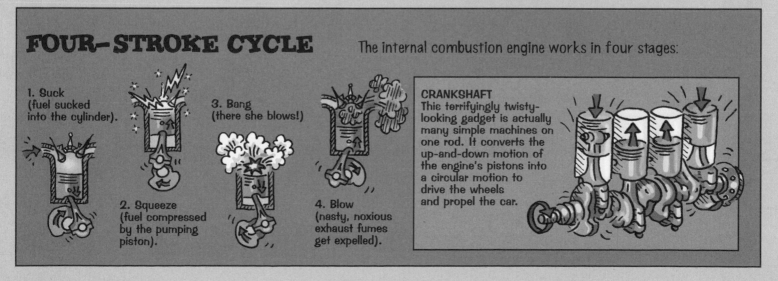

1. Suck (fuel sucked into the cylinder).

2. Squeeze (fuel compressed by the pumping piston).

3. Bang (there she blows!)

4. Blow (nasty, noxious exhaust fumes get expelled).

CRANKSHAFT
This terrifyingly twisty-looking gadget is actually many simple machines on one rod. It converts the up-and-down motion of the engine's pistons into a circular motion to drive the wheels and propel the car.

MAKE A HOVERMONSTER AND CATAPULT

Make use of your most hated CD to create a home-made hovercraft with monstrous results – it's bound to lift your spirits!

You will need:
- an old CD
- a balloon
- a screw top with pull-out nozzle from a sports-type drinks bottle
- Blu-Tack
- a marker pen

1 Take an old CD (or a free sample CD) that you don't want to play any more. Make a ring of Blu-Tack and fix it to the CD, surrounding the hole.

2 Take the screw top from a sports-type drinks bottle – the sort that has a pull-out nozzle. Push this into the ring of Blu-Tack so that it sticks securely. Make sure the hole in the CD isn't blocked.

3 Take a balloon (green is good for monsters – but any colour will do) and draw a monster's face on one side of it using your marker pen.

4 Now blow up the balloon and carefully stretch the open end over the nozzle. Make sure the nozzle is in the closed position, so air cannot escape from the balloon.

58

5 Stand the CD on a smooth surface, so the balloon stands upright. If it flops slightly to one side, re-adjust the neck of the balloon. Holding the bottle top near the Blu-Tack, gently pull up (open) the valve.

6 Let go of your 'hovermonster' and watch as air whooshes out of the balloon, through the hole in the CD and out underneath. The air lifts the CD and the hovercraft floats across the floor as if by magic.

CRUCIAL CATAPULT

Use a simple lever to create a catapult that'll be sure to get you into no end of trouble!

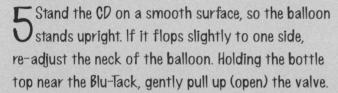

You will need:
- a pencil
- a short ruler
- Blu-Tack
- a piece of paper
- scissors
- sticky tape
- two stacks of books (the same height)
- a large eraser

1 Cut a strip of 2 cm x 12 cm paper. Wind it around your pencil and secure the end to itself (not to the pencil) using sticky tape.

2 Using a blob of Blu-Tack, stick your ruler onto the strip of paper. It MUST be right in the centre of the ruler for it to balance.

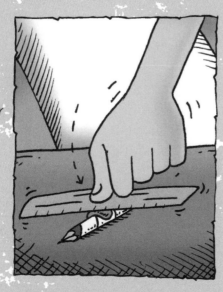

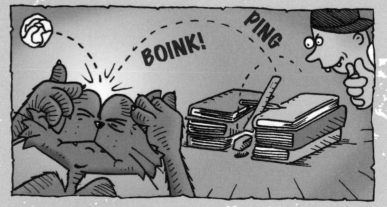

3 Place the ruler between the stacks of books, aiming your 'catapult' in the right direction (at a grumpy friend?) Now put a ball of scrunched-up paper on one end of the ruler, drop your eraser on the other end … FIRE!

PUZZLE ANSWERS

So... are you are a fully-evolved human or a cave-dwelling rock head?
Is your brainbox packed with super cells or is it grinding like a grimy old gearbox?
Are you an amazing mammal or a less than mite-y nit? Let's find out!

HEART TO HEART p19

BLOOD TEST p19

1. a) The four main blood types are: A, B, AB and O.
These were discovered by Karl Landsteiner, an Austrian.
LETTER: T
2. b) Leeches! Yes, these horrible blood-suckers were
often used to get blood out of patients. LETTER: H
3. b) Jellyfish don't have blood. Their cells just absorb
the nutrients and gases they need. LETTER: R
4. c) Platelets stick together like glue wherever there is
a cut. They form a clot, which acts as a protective layer
over your cut, stopping more blood from escaping.
This eventually turns into a scab. LETTER: E
5. a) Valves in the vessels and the heart stop blood doing
a U-turn, by only allowing blood to pass through in one
direction. The blood system wouldn't work properly if
blood was able to flow in any direction! LETTER: E
The letters by the correct answers tell you that leeches
have THREE teeth.

MITE-ILY TRUE OR FLEA-FULLY FALSE? p25

1. FALSE
Fleas don't drink water directly – they absorb
moisture through their shell.

2. TRUE
Fleas can jump about 150 times
their own height.

3. FALSE
Hair lice prefer clean hair
but that's no excuse not
to wash your hair!

4. TRUE
Cat fleas are smaller than dog fleas. And human
fleas are smaller than cat and dog fleas.

5. TRUE
Amazingly, you have mites living in your eyelashes.
They are called follicle mites and they help keep your
eyelashes clean. (Follicles are the narrow tubes in
your skin that hairs grow in.)

6. FALSE
The eggs of head lice are called nits. You nitwit!

TERRIBLE TIMELINE p39

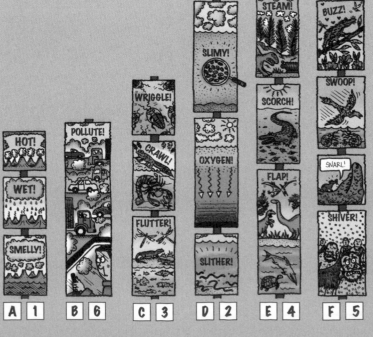

A1   B6   C3   D2   E4   F5

NUMBER CRUNCHING QUIZ p39

1. 1000   2. 200,000   3. 12,000

POSH 'N PARPY MATTER PARTY p44-45

Here are the five rather farty molecules flying around at the Matter Party. Phwoar!

CONFUSING CHEMICALS p49

1. Salt 2. Chalk 3. Talc 4. Vinegar

MACHINE MATCH-UP p55

1-C, 2-E, 3-B, 4-D, 5-A

PEDAL-POWERED PRODUCTS p55

1. TRUE.
Invented by Frenchman François Barathon in Paris, 1895;
2. TRUE.
Another French invention tested in Paris in 1895;
3. FALSE.

PICTURE CREDITS

6, 8 Tony De Saulles; 8–9 Robin Carter; 10–11 Yann le Goaec; 12–13 Tom Connell; 14, 15 Tony De Saulles; 16, 17, 18 Kevin Hopgood; 19 (tr) Gary Northfield, (l, br) Tony De Saulles, (mr) Kevin Hopgood; 20–21 Yann le Goaec; 22, 23, 24 Gary Northfield; 25 (tl, all b) Gary Northfield, (tr) Tony De Saulles; 26–27 Tom Connell; 28–29 Dave Smith; 30, 31 Tony De Saulles; 32, 33 Gemma Hastilow; 34–35 Robin Carter; 36, 37, 38 Dave Smith; 39 Tony De Saulles; 40, 41, 42 Dave Smith; 43 Tony De Saulles; 44–45 Robin Carter; 46–47 Yann le Goaec; 48–49 Gemma Hastilow; 50–51 Yann le Goaec; 52, 53, 54 Dave Smith; 55, 56 Tony De Saulles; 57 Gemma Hastilow; 58, 59 Carl Flint.